WORLD 3-D PHYSICAL MAP

NORTH AMERICA

SOUTH AMERICA

Atlantic Ocean

Pacific Ocean

Greenland

Beaufort Sea

Victoria Is.

Baffin Is.

Baffin Bay

Davis Strait

Denmark St

Ice

BROOKS RANGE

Bering Strait

Yukon

Mackenzie

Great Bear Lake

Great Slave Lake

Hudson Bay

Bering Sea

Gulf of Alaska

Aleutian Is.

Columbia

ROCKY MOUNTAINS

GREAT PLAINS

Missouri

Mississippi

Great Lakes

APPALACHIAN MTS.

Newfoundland

40°N

Colorado

Rio Grande

SIERRA MADRE

Gulf of Mexico

TROPIC OF CANCER

Hawaiian Islands

Caribbean Sea

Galápagos Islands

0° EQUATOR

Orinoco

GUIANA HIGHLANDS

Negro

Amazon

Madeira

São Francisco

Paraná

TROPIC OF CAPRICORN

ANDES MTS.

PAMPAS

40°S

Falkland Islands

Cape Horn

South Georgia

160°W

120°W

80°W

40°W

ANTARCTIC CIRC

Arctic Ocean 40°E 80°E 120°E 160°E 80°N

Svalbard

Novaya Zemlya

Barents Sea Kara Sea Laptev Sea East Siberian Sea

Norwegian Sea ARCTIC CIRCLE

S I B E R I A

N. Dvina Yenisey Lower Tunguska Lena

North Sea Volga URAL MOUNTAINS Ob A S I A Lena Indigirka Kolyma

Baltic Sea Ob Yenisey Angara Aldan

EUROPE Dnieper Don Tobol Irtysh Amur Sea of Okhotsk

ALPS Ural Ishim ALTAY MTS.

Caspian Sea Aral Sea GOBI DESERT Sea of Japan 40°N

Black Sea ZAGROS MTS. Amur

Mediterranean Sea PLATEAU OF TIBET Huang He Yellow Sea

ATLAS MTS. Indus HIMALAYAS Yangtze East China Sea

Nile Red Sea Ganges TROPIC OF CANCER

S A H A R A D E S E R T Arabian Peninsula DECCAN PLATEAU Pacific Ocean

AFRICA Arabian Sea Bay of Bengal South China Sea Philippine Sea

White Nile Gulf of Aden South China Sea

Gulf of Guinea Ubangi Congo ETHIOPIAN HIGHLANDS Celebes Sea

CONGO BASIN Lake Victoria EQUATOR 0°

Kasai

Madagascar Indian Ocean Coral Sea

KALAHARI DESERT GREAT SANDY DESERT

Orange DRAKENSBERG MTS. AUSTRALIA GREAT DIVIDING RANGE TROPIC OF CAPRICORN

Cape of Good Hope New Zealand 40°S

Tasman Sea

0 1000 2000 3000 4000 Miles

0 1000 2000 3000 4000 5000 6000 Kilometers

0° 40°E 80°E 120°E 160°E ANTARCTIC CIRCLE

ANTARCTICA

About the Author

Marie Javins is a writer, comic book editor, and world traveler who, in 2001, made a complete lap around the globe using ships, trains, buses, and other kinds of surface transportation (almost entirely without planes!). She even traveled the whole length of Africa, from Cape Town to Cairo, and wrote a book about it. Since then she has lived in Australia, Spain, Uganda, Namibia, Kuwait, Egypt, New Jersey, and New York. She wrote this book in the last three places on that list, plus Spain!

The maps in this book were developed from base maps created by Mountain High Maps®.
Copyright © 1993 Digital Wisdom®, Inc.
All globe views © Planetary Visions Limited.

Cover design by Annie Tsou.
Book design by Katie Jennings and Annie Tsou.
Geography consultation by Reingard Rohr.
Spot illustrations by Robert Shadbolt.
Typeset in Handwriter & Neutra.
Manufactured in United States.

Library of Congress Cataloging-in-Publication Data available.
ISBN 978-0-8118-6694-1

10 9 8 7 6 5 4 3 2 1

Chronicle Books LLC
680 Second Street, San Francisco, California 94107

www.chroniclekids.com

Photo credits:

Cover: (Chichén Itzá) Dreamstime/Lester Woodward. Page 12: Andrea Menotti. Page 17: Jim Sharp. Page 18: U.S. National Park Service. Page 19: Jim Sharp. Page 20: (Château Frontenac) Dreamstime/Mary Lane. Page 25: (The Great Pyramid of Cholula) Dreamstime/Alexandre Fagundes. Page 26: (El Morro) Dreamstime/Roxana Gonzalez. Page 30: Dreamstime/Alexandre Fagundes. Page 33: (piranha) Dreamstime/Mietitore; (river) Dreamstime/Antonio Negrao. Page 38: (Recoleta cemetery) Dreamstime/Cosmopol. Page 39: Dreamstime/Lee Torrens. Page 40: (man on glacier) Dreamstime/Mercedes Manrique. Page 41: (Leaning Tower of Pisa) Dreamstime/Helen Shore. Page 42: (Duomo) Dreamstime/Kevin Fletcher. Page 45: (view from London Eye) Jim Sharp. Page 47: (Northern Norway at midnight in June) Dreamstime/Kajetan Stozek. Page 52: (Athena) Dreamstime/Volkan Ersoy. Page 53: (distant view) Dreamstime/D. Derics; (close view) Dreamstime/Markz. Page 56: (orangutan) Dreamstime/Bill Kennedy. Page 57: Dreamstime/Regien Paassen. Page 58: Dreamstime/Avner Richard. Page 59: (Ski Dubai images) courtesy of Ski Dubai; (Burj Al-Arab images) courtesy of Burj Al-Arab. Page 61: (full image of Taj Mahal) Clipart.com. Page 62: (Mount Everest) Dreamstime/Jason Maehl. Page 64: (Grand Palace) Dreamstime/Bryan Busovicki. Page 66 (aerial view of Angkor Wat) Dreamstime/Shirley Hu. Page 68: (Mount Fuji) Dreamstime/Thomas Humeau. Page 72: Dreamstime/Tatiana Pavlova. Page 77: Dan Heller. Page 80: (top right) Dreamstime/Hazlan Abdul Hakim. Page 82: Dreamstime/Antoine Beyeler. Page 86: (top right) Dreamstime/David Lloyd; (bottom left) Dreamstime/Christopher Howey. Page 87: courtesy of AJ Hackett Bungy New Zealand. Page 88: (top left) Dreamstime/Astra; (bottom right) Dreamstime/Korostyshevskiy. Page 91: (McMurdo station) Elaine Hood/National Science Foundation; (golf) Robert Schwarz; (penguins) Dreamstime/Goldman.

All other photos: Shutterstock.com.

3-D WORLD

Atlas & Tour

Written by Marie Javins

Map design by
Mapping Specialists, Ltd.

3-D image rendering by
Pinsharp 3-D Graphics

chronicle books·san francisco

CONTENTS

The Statue of Liberty, United States

A cable car in Rio de Janeiro, Brazil

6

▶ **An Atlas Like No Other!** **8**
Meet the Maps 10
How Does 3-D Work? 12

▶ **Welcome to North America!** **13**
North America Political Map 14
North America 3-D Physical Map 15
United States of America
    Political Map 16
The Capitol Building 17
The Grand Canyon 18
New York City 19
Canada Political Map 20
Niagara Falls 21
Polar Bear Country 22
Banff National Park 23
Mexico Political Map 24
Ancient Empires of America 25
Central America &
    Caribbean Political Map 26
Irazú Volcano 27
The Panama Canal 28

▶ **Welcome to South America!** **29**
South America Political Map 30
South America 3-D Physical Map 31
Copacabana Beach 32
The Amazon 33
The Galápagos Islands 34
The Coffee Belt 35
Machu Picchu 36
Buenos Aires 38
Iguazú Falls 39
Tierra del Fuego 40

The Great Pyramids of Giza, Egypt

▶ **Welcome to Europe!** **41**
Europe Political Map.........................42
Europe 3-D Physical Map...................43
United Kingdom Political Map...............44
London...45
Northern Europe Political Map..............46
The Land of the Midnight Sun.................47
Central and Southern Europe
    Political Map................................48
The Eiffel Tower................................49
Rome..50
Prague...51
Athens..52
Sagrada Família Basilica 53
Moscow...54

▶ **Welcome to Asia!** **55**
Asia Political Map.............................56
Asia 3-D Physical Map........................57
Middle East Political Map.....................58
Dubai..59
South Asia Political Map......................60
The Taj Mahal...................................61
Nepal..62
The Himalayas...................................63
Southeast Asia Political Map................64
Singapore..65
The Temples of Angkor.......................66
East Asia Political Map.......................68
Hong Kong.......................................69
The Great Wall of China 70

▶ **Welcome to Africa!** **71**
Africa Political Map...........................72
Africa 3-D Physical Map......................73
The Nile River...................................74
The Great Pyramids...........................75
The Sahara Desert............................76
Timbuktu...77
The Great Rift Valley..........................78
Safari! 79
Cape Town.......................................80

▶ **Welcome to Australia
and Oceania!** **81**
Australia and Oceania Political Map........82
Australasia 3-D Physical Map................83
The Great Barrier Reef........................84
The Wonderful Animals of Oz 85
Rotorua...86
Queenstown.....................................87
Easter Island....................................88

▶ **Welcome to Antarctica!** **89**
Antarctica Political and 3-D
    Physical Maps..............................90
South Pole Science............................91
An Antarctic Ice Cave........................92

▶ **Journey's End** **93**

7

A lion in the African savannah

AN ATLAS LIKE NO OTHER!

Our world is a huge and wonderful place, with almost 200 countries on seven continents as well as countless islands. It would take a lifetime to travel the whole world and see all there is to see.

But there's no need to wait till you're old enough to buy a plane ticket and set off for Timbuktu. That's because you can start exploring the world's cities, countries, islands, and oceans from the comfort of the spot where you're now reading—with the help of this atlas.

Move over, ordinary atlas!

An ordinary atlas has maps (of course!) and some facts and figures, too. These things are important and fascinating, but *this* atlas is special—it'll take you on a 3-D tour around the world! You'll see famous sights across the continents and feel like you've taken a little trip to each place. As you tour through this book, here's what you'll find:

POLITICAL MAPS
These show places created by humans, like countries, states, provinces, cities, and towns.

PHYSICAL MAPS
These show natural features, like mountains, rivers, and deserts. The physical maps in this atlas are very special because they're in 3-D, so you'll see mountains popping off the page.

SPECIAL MAPS
These smaller maps focus on certain information, like the location of ancient ruins in Central America, or the boundaries of the Sahara Desert in Africa.

TOURS

These are visits to some of the world's most interesting places, whether they're ancient sites, big cities, steaming jungles, or parched deserts.

To reach Machu Picchu, many travelers walk the Inca Trail, a four-day hike through the Andes Mountains along an old Incan route. They pass by many other ruins during their walk, and on the fourth day, they are treated to this grand view of Machu Picchu. The ruins you see include residences (both for royals and for workers), temples, and other structures. There was even a system of channels and fountains to provide water to the residences.

3-D POSTCARDS

These photos show you the sights of the world in three dimensions—as close to a real-life view as a book can offer! You'll know to put on your 3-D glasses when you see this symbol:

So, what's on the itinerary?

You'll visit all seven continents—North America, South America, Europe, Asia, Africa, Australia and Oceania, and Antarctica—on your trip around the world. We can't visit *all* the sites on those continents in this book, but we *can* visit plenty of the best ones to give you a good taste of what's out there. You'll have a chance to . . .

- Meet the large, furry inhabitants of the "Polar Bear Capital of the World."
- Marvel at a stunning view of Niagara Falls.
- Tour the tango city—Buenos Aires, Argentina.
- Visit Earth's hottest and coldest deserts.
- Enjoy the beauty of India's exquisite Taj Mahal.
- Explore Angkor Wat, the pride of Cambodia.
- See the ancient sites of Rome and Athens.
- Find out where you can ski on snow in the desert.
- Look down from the world's first bungee jump site.
- And much more!

You won't need your passport for this trip around the world—you'll just need your curiosity, your sense of adventure . . . and, of course, your 3-D glasses! So, bon voyage, traveler. May each step (or turn of the page, in this case) bring a new discovery.

MEET THE MAPS

Here's a quick introduction to the maps in your atlas. The full-page maps come in two varieties: **political** (showing countries, cities, and the like) and **physical** (showing natural features). The **special maps** that accompany the "tour" pages often combine political and physical information.

POLITICAL MAP

COUNTRY NAMES

LINES OF LATITUDE measure location north or south of the **equator**. The equator, which is like an invisible belt around Earth's middle, is 0 degrees (°) latitude. The North Pole is 90° north, and the South Pole is 90° south.

LINES OF LONGITUDE measure location east and west of a line called the prime meridian, which runs through Greenwich, England (the site of an observatory). These lines run from pole to pole.

TERRITORY NAMES This territory is part of the nation listed below.

SPECIAL LATITUDES Some lines of latitude have special names, like the **Tropic of Capricorn** (23.4° south) and the **Tropic of Cancer** (23.4° north). The area between these two lines is a region known as the Tropics. The **Arctic Circle** (66.3° north) and the **Antarctic Circle** (66.3° south) are also important latitude lines.

The **KEY** (sometimes called the **legend**) tells you what the map's symbols mean.

10

Some Natural Features You'll See on Physical Maps

ARCHIPELAGO: A chain of islands

BASIN: The land that water flows across or under on its way to a river

BAY or **GULF:** A body of water that's partly surrounded by land

CAPE or **PENINSULA:** A piece of land that sticks out into water

ESTUARY: A place where a river meets the sea

FJORD: A narrow sea inlet bordered by steep cliffs

ISTHMUS: A strip of land connecting two larger land masses

PLAIN(S): A large area of generally flat land

PLATEAU: A large highland that's mostly flat, like a table

STRAIT: A narrow channel joining two larger bodies of water

3-D PHYSICAL MAP

NATURAL FEATURES are named and described in parentheses when the name doesn't tell you what the feature is. Not sure what **basin** means? Check the glossary above for this and other terms you'll find on physical maps.

All the physical maps are in **3-D**. The 3-D effect makes these mountains appear to rise up from the page. Maps that show the contours of the land are called **relief maps**.

The **SCALE** tells you how much real-world distance is represented by a certain length on the map. Copy the scale onto the edge of a piece of paper, and use the paper like a ruler to measure distances on the map.

11

HOW DOES 3-D WORK?

The image on the right looks flat until you put on your 3-D glasses, and then . . . wow! Suddenly that lion's face sticks out of the page. How does that work?

It's all about making your two eyes see two different things. In real life, when you look around, your eyes see the world from two different angles. Your brain merges these two views, and the differences between them give you a sense of how objects are shaped and how far away they are.

From flat to 3-D!

To make a 3-D image, two images are created: a left-eye image and a right-eye image.

The left-eye image is colored blue, and the right-eye image is colored red. When you put on your 3-D glasses, each eye can only see its own image. Try it! Just put on your 3-D glasses, close your right eye, and look at the red image. It pretty much disappears, right? A similar thing happens if you look at the blue image with your right eye—the blue lens filters out the blue image.

LEFT-EYE IMAGE   **RIGHT-EYE IMAGE**

Can you see very slight differences between these images?

When the two images are placed on top of each other, each eye still only sees its own version of the image. This makes your mind see depth, and there you have it—three dimensions!

Note: For the best view, hold the book vertically and look at the images straight on.

12

Welcome to NORTH AMERICA!

North America—which includes the United States, Canada, Mexico, Central America, and the Caribbean—is the third-largest continent (after Asia and Africa). Most of its population is descended from immigrants who came to the continent during the past 400 years. Today, North America has two of the world's wealthiest nations, the United States and Canada, and U.S. technology and culture have spread all over the world. But there's much more to North America than this. You'll find just a few of the highlights below!

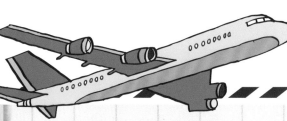

★ More than one grand canyon

The Grand Canyon in the southwestern United States is one of the world's most beautiful canyons. But Mexico's Copper Canyon is four times larger, and you can take a train along its rim!

★ Hustle and bustle

New York City and Mexico City are two of the world's most populated cities. They're diverse, too—people immigrate to these cities from all over the world.

★ Move over, Egypt!

Surprise—the world's largest ancient pyramid isn't in Egypt. It's in Mexico! It's called the Great Pyramid of Cholula, and it was built by the Aztec people. Construction began more than 2,000 years ago.

★ Beary big bears

Polar bears and grizzly bears top the list of the world's biggest bears, and North America has them both.

★ From deep tan to deep freeze!

The Caribbean has some of the world's finest beaches, perfect for tanning and swimming. But if you head way up to the northern parts of Canada and Alaska, you'll find permafrost—which means the ground is frozen year-round!

NORTH AMERICA

POLITICAL MAP

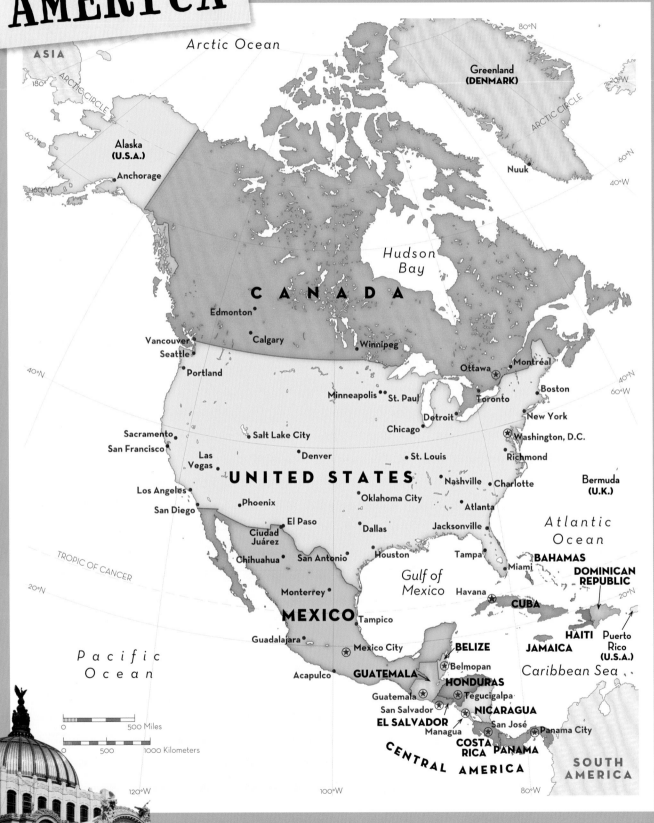

ASIA

Arctic Ocean

ARCTIC CIRCLE

180°

60°N

160°W

Greenland
(DENMARK)

80°N

20°W

ARCTIC CIRCLE

40°W

60°N

Alaska
(U.S.A.)

• Anchorage

Nuuk

Hudson
Bay

C A N A D A

Edmonton •

Vancouver
Seattle •
Portland •

• Calgary

Winnipeg
•

40°N

Minneapolis
•

Ottawa
⊛

Montréal
•

40°N

60°W

• St. Paul

Toronto
•

• Boston

Sacramento •
San Francisco •

Salt Lake City
•

Detroit
•

Chicago
•

• New York

⊛ Washington, D.C.

Las
Vegas •

• Denver

• St. Louis

• Richmond

U N I T E D   S T A T E S

Los Angeles •
San Diego •

• Phoenix

Nashville
•
Oklahoma City
•

• Charlotte
Atlanta
•

Bermuda
(U.K.)

El Paso •

• Dallas

Atlantic
Ocean

Ciudad
Juárez •

Jacksonville
•

Chihuahua •

San Antonio •

Houston
•

TROPIC OF CANCER

20°N

Monterrey •

Tampa
•
Miami •

Gulf of
Mexico

BAHAMAS

DOMINICAN
REPUBLIC

20°N

Havana
⊛ CUBA

MEXICO   Tampico •

HAITI   Puerto
Rico
(U.S.A.)

Guadalajara •

Pacific
Ocean

⊛ Mexico City

Acapulco •

GUATEMALA

BELIZE

⊛ Belmopan

JAMAICA

Caribbean Sea

HONDURAS

Guatemala •
San Salvador •

⊛ Tegucigalpa

EL SALVADOR
Managua
⊛

NICARAGUA

San José
⊛

COSTA
RICA   PANAMA

⊛ Panama City

SOUTH
AMERICA

C E N T R A L   A M E R I C A

120°W

100°W

80°W

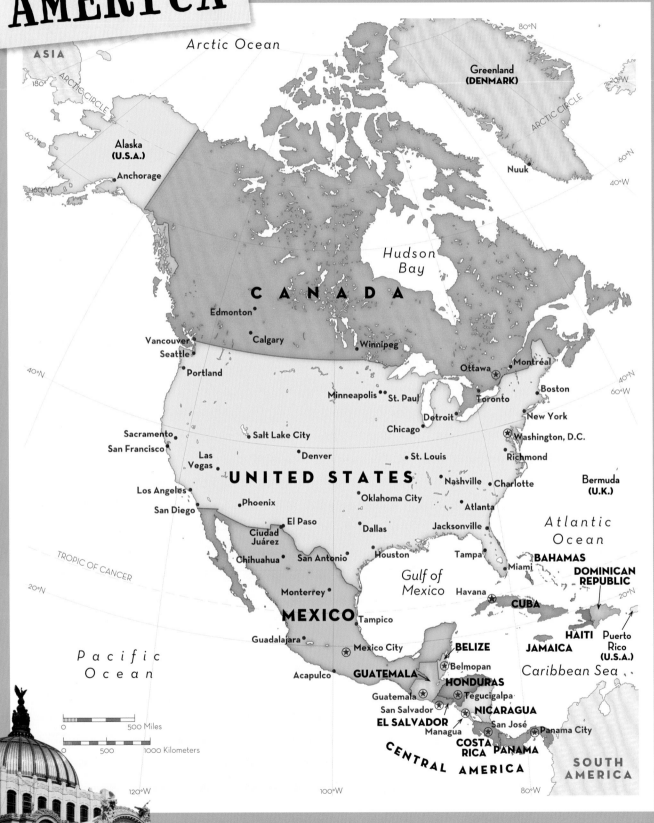
Mexico City's opera house

0   500 Miles

0   500   1000 Kilometers

⊛ National capital

• Other major city

3-D PHYSICAL MAP

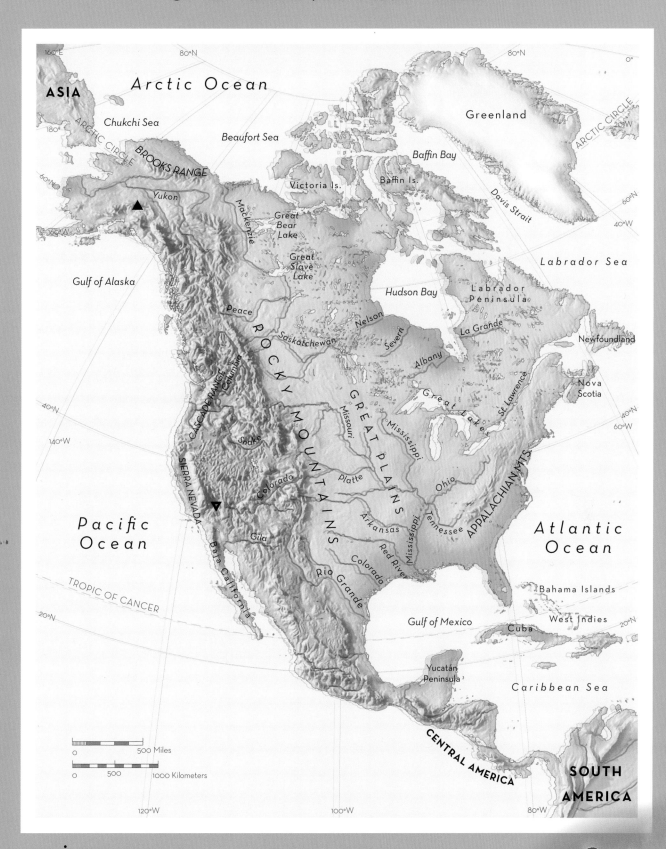

ASIA

Arctic Ocean

Greenland

Chukchi Sea

Beaufort Sea

Baffin Bay

BROOKS RANGE

Yukon

Victoria Is.

Baffin Is.

Davis Strait

Gulf of Alaska

Mackenzie

Great
Bear
Lake

Great
Slave
Lake

Labrador Sea

Hudson Bay

Labrador
Peninsula

Peace

Saskatchewan

Nelson

La Grande

Newfoundland

ROCKY MOUNTAINS

Severn

Albany

Nova
Scotia

Columbia

CASCADE RANGE

Great Lakes

St. Lawrence

Missouri

GREAT PLAINS

Mississippi

Snake

Platte

Ohio

APPALACHIAN MTS.

*Pacific
Ocean*

SIERRA NEVADA

Colorado

Arkansas

Mississippi

Tennessee

*Atlantic
Ocean*

Gila

Red River

Bahama Islands

Baja California

Colorado

Rio Grande

West Indies

TROPIC OF CANCER

Cuba

Gulf of Mexico

Yucatán
Peninsula

Caribbean Sea

CENTRAL AMERICA

SOUTH
AMERICA

0   500 Miles

0   500   1000 Kilometers

160°E   80°N   80°N   0°

ARCTIC CIRCLE   20°W

180°   ARCTIC CIRCLE   60°N

60°N   100°W   40°W

40°N   60°W

140°W

20°N   20°N

120°W   100°W   80°W

MAP
KEY

▲ HIGHEST POINT:
Mount McKinley (Denali), Alaska,
elevation 20,320 feet (6,194 m)

▼ LOWEST POINT:
Death Valley, California,
elevation -282 feet (-86 m)

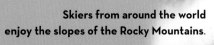

**Skiers from around the world
enjoy the slopes of the Rocky Mountains.**

UNITED STATES OF AMERICA

POLITICAL MAP

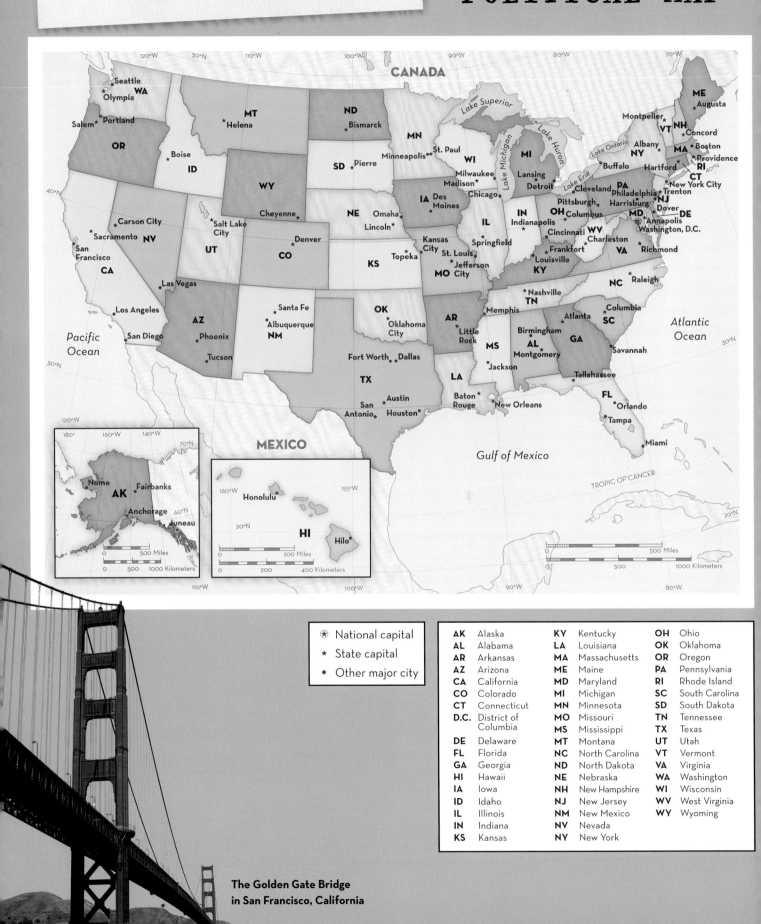

CANADA

Lake Superior
Lake Michigan
Lake Huron
Lake Ontario
Lake Erie

WA Seattle, Olympia
Salem, Portland
OR
Boise **ID**
MT Helena
ND Bismarck
MN St. Paul, Minneapolis
WI Milwaukee, Madison
MI Lansing, Detroit
Montpelier **VT** **NH** Concord
ME Augusta
Albany **NY** Boston **MA**
Buffalo Hartford **CT** Providence **RI**
SD Pierre
WY Cheyenne
Carson City **NV** Salt Lake City **UT** **CO** Denver
Sacramento
San Francisco
CA
Las Vegas
Los Angeles
San Diego
NE Omaha, Lincoln
IA Des Moines
Chicago **IL** Springfield
IN Indianapolis
OH Columbus Cincinnati
Cleveland Pittsburgh **PA** Harrisburg Philadelphia **NJ** Trenton
New York City
Dover **DE**
MD Annapolis Washington, D.C.
WV Charleston Frankfort **KY** Louisville
VA Richmond
NC Raleigh
KS Topeka Kansas City
MO Jefferson City St. Louis
Nashville **TN** Memphis
Columbia **SC**
Atlanta
OK Oklahoma City
Santa Fe **NM** Albuquerque Phoenix **AZ** Tucson
AR Little Rock
MS Jackson **AL** Montgomery Birmingham
GA Savannah
Fort Worth Dallas
TX Austin San Antonio Houston
LA Baton Rouge New Orleans
Tallahassee **FL** Orlando Tampa Miami

Pacific Ocean
Atlantic Ocean
Gulf of Mexico
MEXICO
TROPIC OF CANCER

120°W 110°W 100°W 90°W 80°W 70°W
50°N 40°N 30°N 20°N

AK Nome, Fairbanks, Anchorage, Juneau
180° 160°W 140°W 70°N 60°N
500 Miles
500 1000 Kilometers

HI Honolulu, Hilo
160°W 155°W 20°N
200 Miles
200 400 Kilometers

500 Miles
500 1000 Kilometers

⊛ National capital
★ State capital
• Other major city

AK	Alaska	**KY**	Kentucky	**OH**	Ohio
AL	Alabama	**LA**	Louisiana	**OK**	Oklahoma
AR	Arkansas	**MA**	Massachusetts	**OR**	Oregon
AZ	Arizona	**ME**	Maine	**PA**	Pennsylvania
CA	California	**MD**	Maryland	**RI**	Rhode Island
CO	Colorado	**MI**	Michigan	**SC**	South Carolina
CT	Connecticut	**MN**	Minnesota	**SD**	South Dakota
D.C.	District of Columbia	**MO**	Missouri	**TN**	Tennessee
		MS	Mississippi	**TX**	Texas
DE	Delaware	**MT**	Montana	**UT**	Utah
FL	Florida	**NC**	North Carolina	**VT**	Vermont
GA	Georgia	**ND**	North Dakota	**VA**	Virginia
HI	Hawaii	**NE**	Nebraska	**WA**	Washington
IA	Iowa	**NH**	New Hampshire	**WI**	Wisconsin
ID	Idaho	**NJ**	New Jersey	**WV**	West Virginia
IL	Illinois	**NM**	New Mexico	**WY**	Wyoming
IN	Indiana	**NV**	Nevada		
KS	Kansas	**NY**	New York		

The Golden Gate Bridge in San Francisco, California

3-D POSTCARD

The Capitol Building

Washington, D.C., U.S.A.

⭐ *You'll find Washington, D.C., on the maps on pages 14 and 16.*

WASHINGTON, D.C.
UNITED STATES

The United States Capitol, which sits atop Capitol Hill, is home to both the United States Senate and the House of Representatives—but that's not all! Its familiar dome is also a symbol of American democracy. When construction began in 1793, President George Washington insisted that the building be made of stone, to represent the hope that the American democracy would last a very long time.

THE GRAND CANYON

Arizona, United States

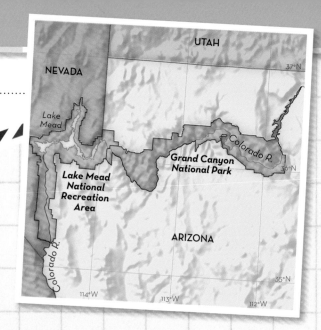

▶ Did one little river really carve out the enormous Grand Canyon, a gorge in Arizona that is over a mile (1.6 km) deep and 277 miles (446 km) long?

Sure did! The Colorado River has been flowing from the Rocky Mountains to the sea for millions of years. That's plenty of time for water, dirt, and sand to erode the rock, especially when Earth's crust is also slowly rising.

Layers of history

The colorful layers of the Grand Canyon are great to look at, but they're also lessons in the earth's history. Each layer is a different type of rock, deposited during a different period. Scientists study the layers to learn about what was happening to the earth over millions of years. Fish and other marine animal fossils show that a shallow sea covered northwestern Arizona millions of years ago!

A long way down and back!

Millions of people visit the Grand Canyon each year. Some go to admire the view and take photos, while others hike, raft, or ride mules into the canyon. Every year hundreds of hikers have to be rescued because they hiked in but grew too exhausted or dehydrated to hike back out. The secret to avoiding this disaster? Plan your route wisely, and take *lots* of water and food.

3-D POSTCARD

New York City
United States

⭐ You'll find New York City on the maps on pages 14 and 16.

New York City is home to the Empire State Building, the United Nations, Wall Street, Broadway, the Statue of Liberty, and more than 8 million people from around the world. Its most famous section, called Manhattan, is shown here. It's built on a small island, and more than 1.5 million people live there.

So where do all those people live and work? Straight up! More than 4,500 skyscrapers, buzzing with people, tower high above the ancient bedrock base of the "city that never sleeps."

CANADA

POLITICAL MAP

Arctic Ocean

400 Miles
400   800 Kilometers

180°
75°N
165°W
150°W
135°W
120°W
105°W
90°W
75°W
60°W
45°W
30°W
15°W
60°N
45°N

ICELAND

Greenland
(DENMARK)

Baffin
Bay

Davis Strait

Beaufort
Sea

Resolute

Atlantic
Ocean

Alaska
(U.S.A.)

Cambridge
Bay

Kugluktuk

Labrador Sea

Dawson
City

YUKON

Iqaluit

Whitehorse

NORTHWEST TERRITORIES

NUNAVUT

Fort
Simpson

Yellowknife

Ivujivik

NEWFOUNDLAND
& LABRADOR

Hudson
Bay

Prince Rupert

Fort
McMurray

Churchill

Fort
Severn

Corner Brook   St. John's

BRITISH
COLUMBIA

ALBERTA

Chisasibi

QUÉBEC

PRINCE
EDWARD
ISLAND

Edmonton

SASKATCHEWAN   MANITOBA

The Pas

Fort Albany

Charlottetown

Vancouver

Saskatoon

ONTARIO

NEW
BRUNSWICK

NOVA
SCOTIA

Victoria

Calgary

Regina

Thunder
Bay

Fredericton

Saint
John

Halifax

Pacific
Ocean

Winnipeg

Sault Ste.
Marie

Montréal

Québec City

UNITED STATES

Lake Superior

Lake Michigan

Lake Huron

Ottawa

Toronto

Lake Ontario

Niagara Falls

Atlantic
Ocean

Windsor

Lake Erie

ARCTIC CIRCLE

> 20

★ National capital

★ Provincial capital

• Other major city

The skyline of Toronto,
Ontario, with the
CN Tower (left)

The Château Frontenac
(a hotel) in Québec City,
Québec

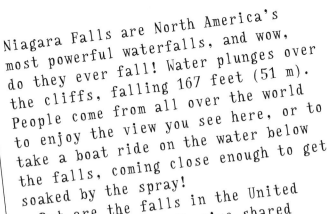

3-D POSTCARD

Niagara Falls
Canada & United States

⭐ You'll find Niagara Falls on the map on page 20, near Lake Ontario.

NIAGARA FALLS
CANADA & UNITED STATES

Niagara Falls are North America's most powerful waterfalls, and wow, do they ever fall! Water plunges over the cliffs, falling 167 feet (51 m). People come from all over the world to enjoy the view you see here, or to take a boat ride on the water below the falls, coming close enough to get soaked by the spray!

But are the falls in the United States or Canada? They're shared between the two countries, between two towns both called...Niagara Falls.

TOUR

POLAR BEAR COUNTRY

Churchill, Manitoba
Canada

▶ The tiny town of Churchill in the Canadian province of Manitoba is invaded by furry white visitors every autumn. And they come hungry! Who are these ravenous invaders? Let's just say there's a reason the sign welcoming visitors to the town says, "The Polar Bear Capital of the World"!

Hungry for Hudson seals

Churchill sits smack-dab on the migration route of hundreds of polar bears, which make beelines for Churchill as soon as its river starts to ice over in October. Why Churchill? Because it's right next to Hudson Bay, a polar bear's favorite restaurant! Polar bears' favorite snacks are seals, which swim in Hudson Bay. All winter, the bears hang out—eating seals—on ice chunks that float south from Churchill. The ice melts in the spring and the bears swim to shore to begin their long walk north—to wait for next October's ice in Churchill.

Quick—call the hotline!

Some polar bears get impatient waiting for the Churchill ice to freeze. They go looking for food in Churchill! Every resident of the town knows the telephone number of the "Polar Bear Hotline," and if they see a polar bear in town, they call the gamekeepers, who capture the bear and give it a time-out before releasing it. Why is everyone so quick to tattle? Because polar bears are not picky. If they can't find a seal, they'll happily eat a human!

3-D POSTCARD

Banff National Park

Alberta, Canada

Banff is Canada's first national park, and its beautiful mountains, valleys, meadows, rivers, lakes, and glaciers attract visitors from all over the world. Here you see Moraine Lake, which is a brilliant shade of blue, thanks to particles of rock in the water. The ground-up rock comes from nearby glaciers that melt into the lake. When light hits the particle-filled water, the result is a beautiful blue color!

MEXICO

POLITICAL MAP

UNITED STATES

Tijuana
Mexicali
Ensenada
Puerto Peñasco
Nogales

BAJA
CALIFORNIA

SONORA
★ Hermosillo
Guaymas

Ciudad
Juárez

Ojinaga

CHIHUAHUA
Chihuahua ★
Delicias

Piedras
Negras

COAHUILA
Monclova ●

Nuevo
Laredo

Santa Rosalía
Gulf of California
Loreto

Ciudad
Obregón
Los
Mochis
SINALOA

Hidalgo
del Parral

NUEVO
LEÓN

BAJA
CALIFORNIA
SUR

Torreón ●
Saltillo ★

Monterrey ★
Matamoros ●

TROPIC OF CANCER

La Paz ★

Culiacán ●
DURANGO
Durango ★

ZACATECAS

Ciudad
Victoria ★

Gulf of Mexico

TROPIC OF CANCER

Cabo San Lucas

Mazatlán ●

Zacatecas ★
SAN LUIS
POTOSÍ

TAMAULIPAS

Ciudad Mante ●

Tampico ●

Pacific
Ocean

NAYARIT
Aguascalientes ★ 1
Tepic ★

San Luis Potosí ★

Chichén
Itzá

Progreso ●
Cancún ●
Mérida ★
Cozumel ●
YUCATÁN

Puerto
Vallarta ●
JALISCO
Guadalajara ★

GUANAJUATO
Guanajuato ★
QUERÉTARO
Querétaro ★
HIDALGO
Pachuca ★

Poza Rica ●

Bay of
Campeche

Campeche ★

QUINTANA
ROO

Colima ●
Manzanillo ●
COLIMA

MICHOACÁN
Morelia ★

Mexico
City ★
Toluca ★ 2

4 Tlaxcala ★
Xalapa ★
Puebla ★
Veracruz ●

Ciudad del
Carmen ●
CAMPECHE

Chetumal ●

Caribbean
Sea

Lázaro Cárdenas ●

MÉXICO
Cuernavaca ★
Taxco ●

3 PUEBLA

VERACRUZ
Coatzacoalcos ●

TABASCO
Villahermosa ★

BELIZE

GUERRERO
Chilpancingo ★

Acapulco ●

OAXACA
Oaxaca ★
Salina
Cruz

Tuxtla
Gutiérrez ★
Comitán ●

CHIAPAS

Gulf of
Tehuantepec

GUATEMALA

Tapachula ●

HONDURAS

EL SALVADOR

0   400 Miles
0   400   800 Kilometers

24

★ National capital
★ State capital
● Other major city

1 AGUASCALIENTES
2 DISTRITO FEDERAL
3 MORELOS
4 TLAXCALA

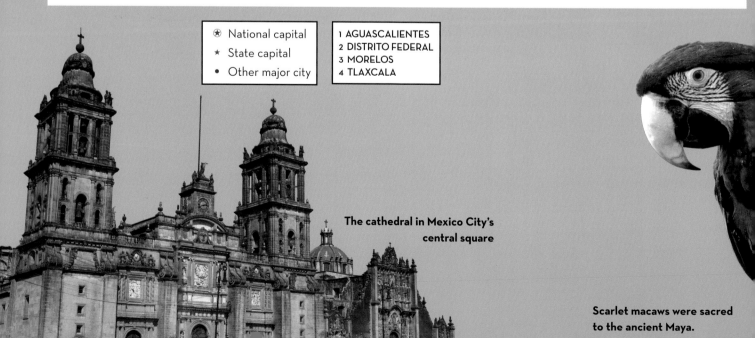

The cathedral in Mexico City's
central square

**Scarlet macaws were sacred
to the ancient Maya.**

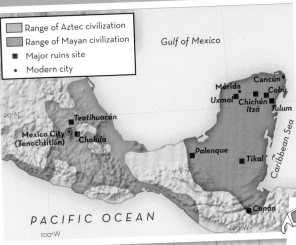

Range of Aztec civilization
Range of Mayan civilization
■ Major ruins site
• Modern city

Gulf of Mexico

Mérida · Cancún
Uxmal · · Cobá
Chichén Itzá · Tulum
20°N
Teotihuacán
Mexico City ⊕
(Tenochtitlán) · Cholula
Palenque
· Tikal
Caribbean Sea
PACIFIC OCEAN
· Copán
100°W
90°W

▶ Great civilizations flourished in the Americas centuries before Europeans discovered the "New World." The ancient Maya—who lived in what is now Mexico and Central America—had writing, books, art, calendars, and complex architecture. They built incredible cities, some parts of which still stand today!

El Castillo

Keep your head!

The most famous Mayan city in Mexico is Chichén Itzá, on the Yucatán Peninsula. Temples, pyramids, and lots of other impressive stone structures can be visited at Chichén Itzá. There are even ball courts!

The Maya were big fans of ball games. Some researchers believe that the Mayan athletes may have paid a big price for losing. One of the wall carvings on Chichén Itzá's ball court suggests that losing players had their heads chopped off!

A snake on the stairs

El Castillo (which means "the castle" in Spanish) is the name of Chichén Itzá's famous pyramid, though it's actually two pyramids, with one inside the other. Twice a year, the sun casts a shadow on the staircase that looks like a serpent creeping up the stairs!

Think big

Even larger than El Castillo, and larger than any ancient pyramid in the world, is the Great Pyramid of Cholula, southeast of Mexico City. Five miles of tunnels wind through Cholula, which was built by ancient people called the Aztecs. It's the largest monument (by volume) anywhere in the world!

A Mayan calendar

The Great Pyramid of Cholula

CENTRAL AMERICA & CARIBBEAN

POLITICAL MAP

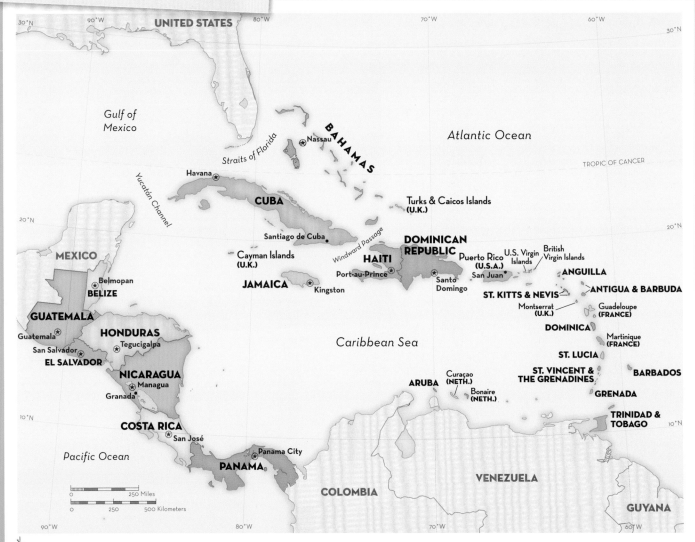

UNITED STATES

Gulf of Mexico

Atlantic Ocean

TROPIC OF CANCER

BAHAMAS
⊛ Nassau

Straits of Florida

Havana

CUBA

Turks & Caicos Islands (U.K.)

MEXICO

Yucatán Channel

Santiago de Cuba

Cayman Islands (U.K.)

Windward Passage

DOMINICAN REPUBLIC

HAITI

Puerto Rico (U.S.A.)

U.S. Virgin Islands

British Virgin Islands

ANGUILLA

Port-au-Prince ⊛

Santo Domingo ⊛

San Juan

ANTIGUA & BARBUDA

JAMAICA

ST. KITTS & NEVIS

Belmopan ⊛

Kingston ⊛

Montserrat (U.K.)

Guadeloupe (FRANCE)

BELIZE

DOMINICA

GUATEMALA

Martinique (FRANCE)

Guatemala ⊛

HONDURAS

Caribbean Sea

ST. LUCIA

San Salvador ⊛

Tegucigalpa ⊛

EL SALVADOR

ST. VINCENT & THE GRENADINES

BARBADOS

NICARAGUA

Managua ⊛

Curaçao (NETH.)

ARUBA

GRENADA

Granada

Bonaire (NETH.)

TRINIDAD & TOBAGO

COSTA RICA

San José ⊛

Panama City ⊛

Pacific Ocean

PANAMA

VENEZUELA

0   250 Miles

COLOMBIA

0   250   500 Kilometers

GUYANA

⊛ National capital
• Other major city

Central America is an isthmus—a thin strip of land connecting two larger landmasses (North and South America).

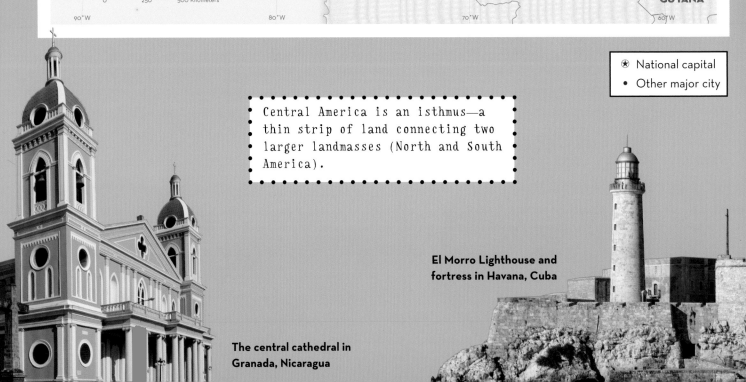

The central cathedral in Granada, Nicaragua

El Morro Lighthouse and fortress in Havana, Cuba

3-D POSTCARD

Irazú Volcano
Costa Rica

Irazú and surrounding volcanoes

Central America has many volcanoes—all part of the Ring of Fire, a zone of active volcanoes around the perimeter of the Pacific Ocean. Irazú is Costa Rica's highest volcano. It erupted in 1963, spewing smoke and ash into the air for two years!

Here you can see Irazú's main crater with its vibrant lake, tinted green by minerals from the volcano. On a clear day (which is rare), you can see both the Atlantic and Pacific Oceans from the top of Irazú!

THE PANAMA CANAL

A Shortcut for Ships

▶ A hundred years ago, if you wanted to sail a ship from New York to San Francisco, it would have taken you *months*. Back then, boats had to sail all the way around the tip of South America. But everyone could see from looking at a map that it was only 50 miles (80 km) from the Atlantic to the Pacific at the narrowest part of Central America. Building a canal as a shortcut for ships between the oceans seemed like a great idea.

Not as easy as it looked

Unfortunately, there were mountains and jungles in the way. And the builders faced dangerous diseases, too!

The French were the first to try to cut a canal—but their effort took the lives of 22,000 men! After two decades, they finally gave up and sold their equipment to American builders, who succeeded by getting rid of disease-carrying mosquitoes and by using some creative engineering.

Tight squeeze!

The Panama Canal was considered large when it was built in 1914, but today's ships are huge, so the canal is now barely wide enough (and it is going to be widened). Locomotives pull ships through the narrowest parts. Only pilots with special training can control ships in the canal—a mistake could get a ship stuck!

Each ship pays a toll, based on weight, to cross the Panama Canal. The smallest toll ever paid was 36 cents—by a swimmer named Richard Halliburton in 1928!

A view from a boat in the canal

28

Welcome to SOUTH AMERICA!

From Brazil's sunny beaches to the icy glaciers of southern Chile, South America has a lot to offer a traveler. Parts of this triangular continent sit in the northern hemisphere, but most of it falls south of the equator. It's famous for grassy plains and open sky in Argentina, the Amazon rain forest of Brazil, and plentiful oil in Venezuela. It also has the world's highest capital city, in Bolivia. Below you'll find a few more highlights to start your tour of South America!

★ That's one skinny country!

The world's longest mountain range, the Andes, runs along the west coast of South America, forming Chile's natural border and making it one of the oddest-shaped countries on Earth.

★ Cities in the clouds

The Incas had an empire in Peru about 500 years ago. Today, travelers can hike to their mountaintop cities along the same roads and trails the Incas used.

★ Water wonders

The world's tallest waterfall, Angel Falls, is in Venezuela, and perhaps the world's most dramatic falls, Iguazú Falls, sits on the border between Argentina and Brazil. The world's second-longest river—the Amazon—runs through Peru, Colombia, and Brazil.

★ A pink dolphin?

South America's Amazon River is home to some unusual creatures, like pink dolphins and aquatic anaconda snakes. Another part of South America—the Galápagos Islands—is home to animals famous for not being afraid of humans!

SOUTH AMERICA

POLITICAL MAP

Caribbean Sea

Barranquilla
Maracaibo
Caracas

VENEZUELA

Atlantic
Ocean

10°N

Medellín

Georgetown
Paramaribo

Bogotá

GUYANA

French Guiana
(FRANCE)

COLOMBIA

SURINAME

Cali

Macapá

EQUATOR

EQUATOR

Quito

Belém
São Luís

ECUADOR

Manaus

Fortaleza

PERU

B R A Z I L

Recife

10°S

10°S

Lima

Salvador

La Paz

Brasília

BOLIVIA

Sucre

Belo Horizonte

PARAGUAY

São Paulo
Rio de Janeiro

20°S

20°S

TROPIC OF CAPRICORN

CHILE

Asunción

Santos

TROPIC OF CAPRICORN

Pacific
Ocean

ARGENTINA

Pôrto Alegre

Córdoba

URUGUAY

30°S

30°S

Rosario
Buenos Aires

Montevideo

La Plata

Santiago

Mar del Plata

Atlantic Ocean

40°S

40°S

500 Miles

0   500   1000 Kilometers

Falkland Islands
(U.K.)

South Georgia
(U.K.)

50°S

The famous opera house
in Buenos Aires, Argentina

Note: Bolivia has two
capitals because the
branches of the government
are in different cities.

⊛ National capital
• Other major city

3-D PHYSICAL MAP

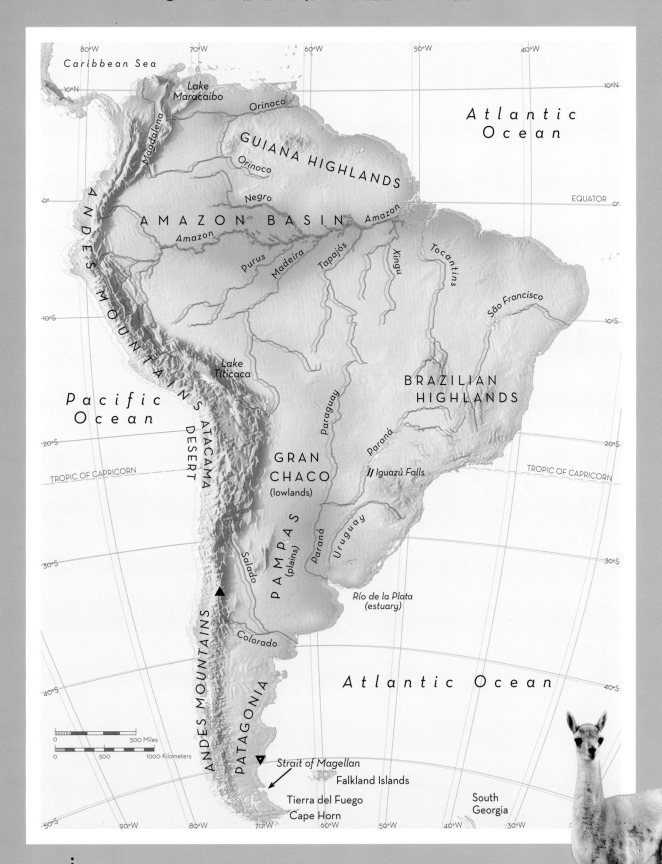

Caribbean Sea

10°N

Lake
Maracaibo

Orinoco

Atlantic
Ocean

Magdalena

GUIANA HIGHLANDS

Orinoco

10°N

80°W

70°W

60°W

50°W

40°W

Negro

EQUATOR

0°

A M A Z O N   B A S I N

Amazon

Amazon

0°

Purus

Madeira

Tapajós

Xingu

Tocantins

São Francisco

A N D E S   M O U N T A I N S

10°S

10°S

Lake
Titicaca

Pacific
Ocean

BRAZILIAN
HIGHLANDS

ATACAMA DESERT

Paraguay

20°S

20°S

GRAN
CHACO
(lowlands)

Paraná

Iguazú Falls

TROPIC OF CAPRICORN

TROPIC OF CAPRICORN

P A M P A S
(plains)

Paraná

Uruguay

Salado

30°S

Río de la Plata
(estuary)

30°S

ANDES MOUNTAINS

Colorado

Atlantic Ocean

40°S

40°S

PATAGONIA

0   500 Miles

Strait of Magellan

0   500   1000 Kilometers

Falkland Islands

Tierra del Fuego
Cape Horn

South
Georgia

50°S

90°W

80°W

70°W

60°W

50°W

40°W

30°W

31

MAP KEY

▲ **HIGHEST POINT:**
Mount Aconcagua, Argentina,
elevation 22,834 feet (6,960 m)

▼ **LOWEST POINT:**
Laguna del Carbón,
elevation -344 feet (-105 m)

**Llamas live in the
Andes Mountains.**

3-D POSTCARD
Copacabana Beach
Rio de Janeiro, Brazil

★You'll find Rio de Janeiro on the map on page 30.

Copacabana Beach in Rio de Janeiro, 2.5 miles (4 km) long, sits beside a street of fancy hotels, shops, and restaurants. This is one of the world's most famous beaches, and there is always something happening day and night, whether it's volleyball, eating, sunbathing, or just plain old swimming.

RIO DE JANEIRO
BRAZIL

▶ The Amazon River snakes across South America from high in the Andes Mountains all the way to the sea in Brazil. The banks are lined with the world's largest rain forest, a humid jungle full of exotic trees and plants that produce 20 percent of the world's oxygen.

Amazon animals

The second-longest river in the world is famous for more than its rain forest. Amazon wildlife includes some of the most unique animals in the world. In Peru, there is a giant river otter, which can grow to be 6 feet (about 2 m) long!

Another animal found in the area is the capybara (ka-pee-BARE-uh), a rodent that looks like a giant guinea pig—it's about 4 feet (1.2 m) long! Some people eat capybara, and in Peru and Bolivia, guinea pigs are also common snacks. The Amazon River itself hosts unusual fish and wildlife, including

A piranha!

33

meat-eating piranha fish, a pink river dolphin called a boto, and the famous anaconda snake.

Rain forest in trouble

The Amazon rain forest is the largest rain forest in the world, but it gets smaller every day due to agriculture, logging, and cattle grazing. This is called deforestation, and it's a big concern, since it harms a forest that generates so much oxygen and hosts so many unique species of plants and animals. But the forest does have help—from conservationists and scientists who are working hard to keep it thriving.

TOUR

THE GALÁPAGOS ISLANDS

Ecuador

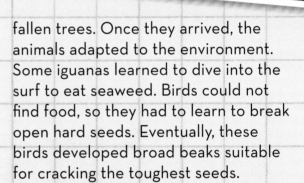

34

▶ Swimming iguanas. Tortoises the weight of three men. Dancing birds with bright blue feet. Sea lions so fearless that they waddle right up to people and sniff them. They all live in the Galápagos Islands.

Sometimes called the Enchanted Islands, the Galápagos Islands sit in the Pacific Ocean off the coast of Ecuador (and the islands are part of Ecuador). Hundreds of animals found nowhere else in the world call this cluster of islands home.

Adapt to survive

All of the islands in the Galápagos chain were pushed up out of the ocean millions of years ago by volcanic activity. The island's animals arrived by air and by sea—maybe by swimming or by floating on

fallen trees. Once they arrived, the animals adapted to the environment. Some iguanas learned to dive into the surf to eat seaweed. Birds could not find food, so they had to learn to break open hard seeds. Eventually, these birds developed broad beaks suitable for cracking the toughest seeds.

When Charles Darwin, a geologist, visited the Galápagos Islands in 1835, he realized that the animals had changed based on their environment. This led to his famous books about evolution.

Not afraid of people

Touching the animals is strictly forbidden in the Galápagos Islands. But sometimes the animals don't follow the rules and approach humans. Why? Because there were no humans on the islands for thousands of years, so the animals never learned to be afraid of them!

A blue-footed booby

For millions around the world, the morning begins with a cup (or two!) of coffee. But where does all this coffee come from? About half of it comes from South America, and a third of that is grown in Brazil. The rest of South America's coffee comes from Ecuador, Colombia, Venezuela, Peru, and Bolivia.

The bean belt

Coffee grows best in tropical climates, in hilly places with some shade, reliable rain, and rich soil. There is a region called "the bean belt" around Earth's middle where coffee grows well. Different conditions produce different types of coffee, so Brazilian coffee tastes different from Peruvian or Colombian coffee. Even within Brazil, there are three growing regions with slight variations in conditions.

Some huge companies grow coffee on tremendous plantations where machines pick the coffee berries (whose seeds are what we call coffee beans), but there are also plenty of small farms run by families who pick each berry by hand. After harvest, the beans are roasted, turning them dark brown like the ones on the right. Then the beans can be ground to make coffee.

Check out these life-size beans with your 3-D glasses!

Top-secret mission

Even though so much coffee is grown in South America, coffee drinking wasn't even invented there! It started in Ethiopia and Yemen, then was adopted throughout the Middle East and Europe. The French brought it to their colonies in the Caribbean, but it took a Brazilian military officer on a secret coffee-acquiring mission to steal coffee beans and plants from the French and bring them home to Brazil in 1727.

35

MACHU PICCHU

Peru

Llamas at Machu Picchu

▶ Nicknamed the "Lost City of the Incas," the ruins of Machu Picchu (MAH-choo PEE-choo, meaning "Old Peak") were never really lost. The city's builders, the Incas, carefully chose a location that was naturally hidden on a mountain overlooking a remote valley.

How come they chose somewhere so inconvenient? It's believed that Machu Picchu—built in 1440—was a retreat for royalty of the Incan empire, not a working city. The nobility would have wanted privacy in an area with natural defenses, and perhaps they also liked the beautiful scenery of the steep mountains.

"Lost" and found

When the Spanish invaded Peru in 1532, they never found Machu Picchu, and no Incas mentioned that it existed. In time, only local people living in or near the ruins knew there was a mountaintop fortress high in the Andes.

Four centuries later, in 1911, an American archaeologist named Hiram Bingham was searching for a different Incan city when Quechuans—descendants of the Incas—led him to Machu Picchu. He was so amazed by its temples, terraces, houses, and other structures that he wrote a book about it. *National Geographic* magazine then featured the ruins, and they became world famous.

No cement required

Today Machu Picchu is the most visited archaeological site in South America. Tourists get to visit lots of original buildings, still standing because the Incas were such great architects. The building blocks fit so tightly together that cement was not needed—not even a knife can fit between them!

3-D POSTCARD

Machu Picchu

Peru

To reach Machu Picchu, many travelers walk the Inca Trail, a four-day hike through the Andes Mountains along an old Incan route. They pass by many other ruins during their walk, and on the fourth day, they are treated to this grand view of Machu Picchu. The ruins you see include residences (both for royals and for workers), temples, and other structures. There was even a system of channels and fountains to provide water to the residences!

TOUR

BUENOS AIRES

Argentina

Recoleta cemetery

Argentina's capital, Buenos Aires, is a city so dazzling that people often compare it to Paris.

It's one of the wealthiest and most fashionable cities in South America, and its architecture appears European—but Buenos Aires is uniquely Argentine. The city is home to colorful *barrios* (the Spanish word for "neighborhoods"), the tango dance, famous steak dinners, and an incredible cemetery called Recoleta that is a tourist attraction in its own right!

Pricey plots

Argentines sometimes joke that it is cheaper to live extravagantly when alive than to get into the expensive mausoleums in Recoleta after death. The Gothic cemetery contains thousands of marble graves, all ornately designed in various styles resembling mansions, pyramids, chapels, and Greek temples.

But Buenos Aires is known for more than just its incredible cemetery. It features grand boulevards, museums, colonial neighborhoods, and a renowned opera house.

A perfect port

People from Buenos Aires are called *porteños* (por-TAIN-yos), which means "people of the port." Buenos Aires became famous for its port because it was in a good location for trading between South America and Europe.

But Buenos Aires's location didn't only bring in trade—it also brought in European culture, like art and music. *Porteños* loved opera performances so much that in 1908—after 20 years of building—they opened Teatro Colón, a huge opera house that holds around 3,000 people. Its classic look and great sound quality are famous all over the world.

3-D POSTCARD

Iguazú Falls
Brazil & Argentina

⭐ You'll find Iguazú Falls on the maps on pages 31 and 38.

IGUAZÚ FALLS
BRAZIL
&
ARGENTINA

The huge cascades of horseshoe-shaped Iguazú Falls form some of the most amazing waterfalls on earth. There are about 270 different drops, with the tallest being 263 feet (80 m). That's a lot of water pouring across the cliffs on the border between Argentina and Brazil! Iguazú means "big water," and these falls are so big that visitors have to check the falls out from both countries to get a really good look.

TIERRA DEL FUEGO

Chile and Argentina

At the southern tip of South America, in a region called Patagonia, there's a cluster of islands whose name is Spanish for "land of fire."

But Tierra del Fuego does not have fires raging across it. It's not even hot! So how did this chilly archipelago (chain of islands) get its name? It's said that when the first Europeans saw the area, they saw bonfires on the shore. These were used by the native tribes to keep warm, but it looked like the land was full of fire.

Lots and lots of ice

No one makes fires today, because it's easier to go inside and turn on the heat. And they need the heat just like the natives needed fire, because it's chilly in southern Patagonia. It's so cold, in fact, that one of the biggest tourist attractions in Patagonia is Los Glaciares National Park, a massive ice field that features 47 huge glaciers! Glaciers are tremendous buildups of ice that slowly move downhill, pulled by gravity.

Most tourists like to visit the Perito Moreno Glacier (named for an explorer) the best, because it is so active. Every few years, a piece of the glacier cracks and collapses off its edge with a huge BOOM! This hardly makes a dent in the glacier—it's almost 100 square miles (250 square km) of ice!

Smaller pieces fall off all the time. This is called calving, and it's how icebergs are created. Even when the glacier doesn't calve, it creaks and moans from the pressure of more ice slowly sliding downward!

Perito Moreno Glacier

40

Welcome to EUROPE!

Europe is the second-smallest continent, but it seems to have a bigger presence in the world because European culture has spread all over the globe. Centuries ago, European countries colonized other areas. Also, during times of war or hardship, Europeans left to seek better lives elsewhere. These days, Europe is a very nice place to live, so people are more likely to move *there* than to move *away*. It's also a very popular place to travel. See what you think when you take your tour!

★ Many mountains

Much of Europe is covered in mountains, which acted as natural barriers for centuries, allowing many different cultures and languages to develop. Europe's most famous mountain range is the Alps.

★ New nations

Eastern European countries such as Ukraine, Belarus, and Moldova still struggle to gain strong economies after years under the rule of the Soviet Union—a nation that has since broken up into smaller countries, the largest of which is Russia.

★ Midnight sun

The five Nordic countries—Norway, Sweden, Finland, Denmark, and Iceland—can be really cold in the winter, but they have beautiful, bright (yet short) summers. In the northernmost places, the sun shines at midnight during part of the summer!

★ You're on the wrong side of the road!

In Great Britain, Ireland, Malta, and Cyprus, they drive on the *left* side of the road, while in the rest of Europe, they drive on the *right*. This makes for some interesting travels when drivers take their cars on vacation.

EUROPE

POLITICAL MAP

ICELAND

ARCTIC CIRCLE

Norwegian
Sea

SWEDEN

FINLAND

R U S S I A

ASIA
EUROPE

NORWAY

Northern
Ireland
Scotland

North
Sea

ESTONIA

Baltic Sea

LATVIA

IRELAND

UNITED
KINGDOM

DENMARK

Kaliningrad
(RUSSIA)

LITHUANIA

Wales

England

BELARUS

KAZAKHSTAN

Atlantic
Ocean

NETHERLANDS

BELGIUM

GERMANY

POLAND

LUXEMBOURG

CZECH REP.

SLOVAKIA

UKRAINE

LIECHTENSTEIN

SWITZERLAND

AUSTRIA

HUNGARY

MOLDOVA

Caspian Sea

FRANCE

ITALY

SLOVENIA

CROATIA

ROMANIA

BOSNIA &
HERZEGOVINA

Black Sea

GEORGIA

PORTUGAL

SPAIN

MONACO

ANDORRA

SAN MARINO

SERBIA

KOSOVO

BULGARIA

AZERBAIJAN

VATICAN CITY

MONTENEGRO

MACEDONIA

TURKEY

ALBANIA

TURKEY

Mediterranean Sea

GREECE

AFRICA

ASIA

500 Miles

500

1000 Kilometers

MALTA

CYPRUS

The Duomo (a cathedral)
in Florence, Italy

Neuschwanstein Castle
in Germany

3-D PHYSICAL MAP

32°W · 24°W · 16°W · 8°W · 0° · 8°E · 16°E · 24°E · 32°E · 40°E · 48°E

Iceland

ARCTIC CIRCLE

Norwegian Sea

Shetland Islands

North Sea

British Isles

Atlantic Ocean

Bay of Biscay

PYRENEES MTS.

Iberian Peninsula

Strait of Gibraltar

Douro

Tagus

Ebro

Balearic Is.

Corsica

Sardinia

Sicily

M e d i t e r r a n e a n   S e a

AFRICA

English Channel

Thames

Seine

Loire

Rhine

Rhône

A L P S

APENNINE MTS.

Po

Adriatic Sea

Ionian Sea

Elbe

Oder

Vistula

Danube

Danube

CARPATHIAN MTS.

Balkan Peninsula

Aegean Sea

Crete

Scandinavia

Baltic Sea

Western Dvina

Prypyats

Dniester

Dnieper

Desna

Don

Northern Dvina

Sukhona

Volga

Volga

Ural

Black Sea

CAUCASUS MTS.

Caspian Sea

URAL MOUNTAINS

ASIA
EUROPE

ASIA

58°N · 50°N · 42°N · 34°N

500 Miles
500   1000 Kilometers

The continent of Europe is really part of the landmass of Asia. The accepted border between Europe and Asia follows the line shown on this map, along the Ural Mountains, the Ural River, the Caucasus Mountains, the Caspian Sea, and the Black Sea. The border runs through some countries, like Russia and Turkey, so these countries have a "European" part and an "Asian" part.

MAP KEY

▲ **HIGHEST POINT:**
Mount Elbrus, Russia,
elevation 18,510 feet (5,642 m)

▼ **LOWEST POINT:**
Caspian Sea,
elevation -92 feet (-28 m)

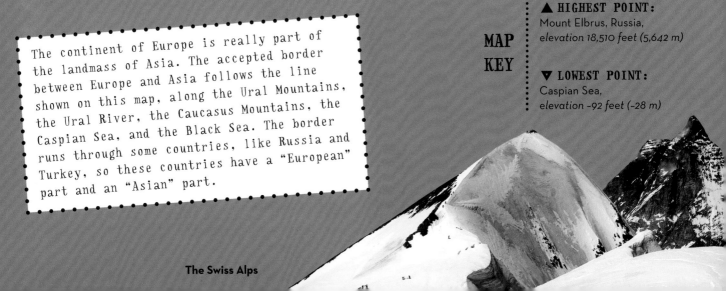

The Swiss Alps

UNITED KINGDOM

POLITICAL MAP

60°N
Shetland Islands
Orkney Islands
Isle of Lewis
Isle of Skye
Atlantic Ocean
Scotland
Aberdeen
Dundee
Perth
Dunfermline
Glasgow
Greenock
Edinburgh
Motherwell
North Sea
55°N
Londonderry
Northern Ireland
Belfast
Lisburn
Carlisle
Newcastle
Scarborough
IRELAND
Dublin
Isle of Man
Irish Sea
England
Kingston upon Hull
Leeds
Manchester
Liverpool
Sheffield
Wrexham
Nottingham
Leicester
Aberystwyth
Birmingham
Norwich
Coventry
Wales
Stratford upon Avon
St. George's Channel
Swansea
Cardiff
Oxford
London
Bristol
Canterbury
Salisbury
Southampton
Brighton
Portsmouth
Plymouth
Celtic Sea
Channel Islands
English Channel
FRANCE
50°N

0   100 Miles
0   100   200 Kilometers

Edinburgh Castle in Edinburgh, Scotland

⊛ National capital
★ Regional capital
• Other major city

Stonehenge, an ancient monument
near Salisbury, England

44

A view of the Houses of Parliament from the London Eye

The London Eye

▶ A great way to start a visit to London, the capital city of the United Kingdom, would be to take a ride on one of London's famous red double-decker buses. But be sure to get off the bus when you roll past the Houses of Parliament on the River Thames. You'll know you're there when you see the enormous clock tower at one end of the building—it's called Big Ben!

Why name a clock Ben?

People call the whole tower Big Ben, but Big Ben is actually the main bell inside the clock, called the Great Clock of Westminster. The bell weighs as much as 145 men! People disagree about how Big Ben was named, but some think it was named after Sir Benjamin Hall, a lawmaker who gave the order to make the bell in 1856.

Big Ben is so famous because it's incredibly reliable and its chime has heralded nearly every hour since September 1859. It also has a special importance because the building it's attached to—the Houses of Parliament—is the center of British government. Big Ben isn't just a clock. It's a symbol of a country.

What else is there to see?

Lots! There's Piccadilly Circus, a busy area (not really a circus) with neon signs and sidewalks packed with crowds pouring in and out of nearby shops. There are plenty of museums, including the Tower of London, where you can see the Crown Jewels. And to get a bird's-eye view of the city, hop aboard the London Eye, a giant observation wheel beside the river. Check out the view above!

Big Ben

NORTHERN EUROPE

POLITICAL MAP

ICELAND

⊛ Reykjavík

0 — 100 Miles
0 — 100 — 200 Kilometers

ARCTIC CIRCLE

70°N

Tromsø

RUSSIA

Narvik

Kiruna •
Gällivare

Bodø •

Rovaniemi

ARCTIC CIRCLE

Moi Rana •

Luleå •
Oulu •

0 — 200 Miles
0 — 200 — 400 Kilometers

Atlantic Ocean

Umeå •

FINLAND

SWEDEN

Trondheim •

Vaasa •

Kuopio •

46

Sundsvall •

Tampere •
Lahti •

NORWAY

Bergen •

Turku •

60°N

Gävle •

Helsinki ⊛

60°N

Oslo ⊛

Västerås • Uppsala •
Örebro • Stockholm ⊛

Tallinn ⊛

ESTONIA

RUSSIA

Tartu •

Kristiansund •

Norrköping •

Jönköping •

Riga ⊛

Göteborg •

LATVIA

Ålborg •

Liepaja •

Daugavpils •

Århus •

Baltic Sea

DENMARK

Copenhagen ⊛

Klaipéda •

Odense • Malmö •

LITHUANIA

Kaunas •

GERMANY

Vilnius ⊛

BELARUS

10°E

POLAND

RUSSIA

20°E

⊛ National capital

• Other major city

Stockholm, Sweden

THE LAND OF THE MIDNIGHT SUN

Northern Scandinavia & Russia

Northern Norway at midnight in June!

Fjords in northern Norway

▶ In the northernmost parts of Europe, above the Arctic Circle, the sun shines all night during the summer! Most of the year, this region—which includes parts of Norway, Sweden, Finland, and Russia—is a chilly place, but summertime means all-night volleyball games or midnight miniature golf!

Sunny all night?

From late May to early July, the top of our planet tilts toward the sun. That's why it's warm in the Northern Hemisphere for those months. The *very* top part of our planet is *always* facing the sun during that time—so there's no night up there. The sun just never sets! It's called the season of the midnight sun. (Down at the South Pole during that time, it's the opposite—it's *always* night.)

The season of the midnight sun doesn't last long. Summer nights gradually brighten starting in the middle of May and remain light for about two and a half months. The sun is up for the longest time at the end of June—a time called midsummer.

Bring your swimsuit!

People who live near the Arctic Circle are used to sleeping in sunlight, but visitors often struggle because the days never seem to end. Why sleep when you could be at one of Sweden's warmest beaches—Pite Havsbad (PETE-eh HOVE-es-baad)—or playing soccer with friends?

Other places that are above the Arctic Circle have midnight sun, too, like Alaska, Canada, Iceland, and Greenland. The same thing happens under the Antarctic Circle, but no one lives there. But the penguins and seals down there surely enjoy the long days of polar summers!

Reindeer live in this part of the world.

CENTRAL & SOUTHERN EUROPE

POLITICAL MAP

North Sea
Baltic Sea
Celtic Sea
Atlantic Ocean
Bay of Biscay
Adriatic Sea
Balearic Sea
Tyrrhenian Sea
Ionian Sea
Aegean Sea
Black Sea
Mediterranean Sea

IRELAND
UNITED KINGDOM
DENMARK
SWEDEN
LATVIA
LITHUANIA
RUSSIA
BELARUS
NETH.
BEL.
LUX.
GERMANY
POLAND
UKRAINE
LIECH.
CZECH REPUBLIC
SLOVAKIA
AUSTRIA
HUNGARY
MOLDOVA
FRANCE
SWITZ.
SLOVENIA
CROATIA
SAN MARINO
ROMANIA
SERBIA
B & H
MONACO
ANDORRA
ITALY
MONT.
KOS.
BULGARIA
MAC.
TURKEY
ALB.
GREECE
VATICAN CITY
PORTUGAL
SPAIN
MALTA
CYPRUS
MOROCCO
ALGERIA
TUNISIA
LIBYA
EGYPT
RUSSIA

Amsterdam • The Hague • Brussels • Hamburg • Berlin • Gdańsk • Bydgoszcz • Warsaw • Vitsyebsk • Minsk • Homyel • Kharkiv • Kiev • Donetsk • Dnipropetrovsk • Frankfurt • Wiesbaden • Łódź • Wrocław • Kraków • Prague • Paris • Strasbourg • Stuttgart • Munich • Vienna • Bratislava • Budapest • Chisinau • Odesa • Nantes • Zürich • Bern • Lyon • Ljubljana • Milan • Venice • Zagreb • Bucharest • Genoa • Belgrade • Sarajevo • Bilbao • Toulouse • Nice • Podgorica • Pristina • Sofia • Istanbul • Marseille • Corsica • Tirana • Thessaloniki • Ankara • Porto • Valladolid • Zaragoza • Barcelona • Madrid • Rome • Naples • Athens • Nicosia • Lisbon • Valencia • Sardinia • Skopje • Seville • Málaga • Gibraltar (U.K.) • Palermo • Sicily • Catania • Crete • Valletta

48

200 Miles
0   200   400 Kilometers

Legend:
⊛ National capital
● Other major city
○ Small country

ALB.	ALBANIA
B & H	BOSNIA & HERZEGOVINA
BEL.	BELGIUM
KOS.	KOSOVO
LIECH.	LIECHTENSTEIN
LUX.	LUXEMBOURG
MAC.	MACEDONIA
MONT.	MONTENEGRO
NETH.	NETHERLANDS
SWITZ.	SWITZERLAND

Belvedere Palace in Vienna, Austria

3-D POSTCARD

The Eiffel Tower
Paris, France

★ You'll find Paris on the map on page 48.

The Eiffel Tower—named for its builder, Alexandre Gustave Eiffel—is one of the world's most famous landmarks.

But when the Eiffel Tower was built in 1889, it was supposed to be a temporary exhibit for a World's Fair—it was to stand for only 20 years. And the French public hated the way it looked! Fortunately, the Eiffel Tower was useful for radio broadcasting, and it grew on the public. By the time the 20 years was up, it would have been unthinkable to tear the tower down.

What's it like to look down from the Eiffel Tower? Check out the view!

TOUR

ROME

Italy

Inside the Colosseum

▶ Italy's capital city, Rome, is a hodgepodge of history, style, art, and culture that developed over 3,000 years. There are hundreds of ancient sites in Rome. One of the most famous ruins is called the Colosseum. It's almost 2,000 years old!

What's the Colosseum, anyway?

The Colosseum is an outdoor stadium, like a place where you'd see a football game today. It's shaped like a giant stone doughnut with the playing field in the hole. Just as in today's stadiums, the cheapest seats were at the top. The Colosseum was used for drama, sports, fake sea battles, executions, and, most famously, for gladiator combat. Imagine a crowd of 50,000 people cheering on the gladiators as they fought each other or a hungry lion!

Huge city, huge empire

Right down the street from the Colosseum stands the Roman Forum. That's where the Roman Empire was centered 2,000 years ago. In its day, Rome was the biggest city the western world had ever known, and it was governed from here, among the columns, temples, and halls of the Roman Forum.

Ancient Rome's markets, government buildings, and schools would have been buzzing with politicians, students, priests, and shoppers, all believing that the Roman Empire would never crumble. That's because, at its height, the empire covered much of Europe, parts of North Africa, and even some of Asia—all the way to the Persian Gulf.

Eventually, though, the empire did decline, about 1,500 years ago, and historians still argue over exactly why. But the city of Rome, known as the "Eternal City," continued to thrive. It's still an important city today!

One of the many ruins of the Roman Forum

The Colosseum

50

3-D POSTCARD

Prague
Czech Republic

⭐ *You'll find Prague on the map on page 48.*

PRAGUE
CZECH
REPUBLIC

Prague, a city of 1.2 million people, is the capital of the Czech Republic. Its stunning medieval center is one of the best-preserved old cities of Europe because it was not heavily damaged during World War II, as so many other cities were. Tourists love to go to Prague to walk the cobblestone streets among the historic buildings. There's even a 1,100-year-old castle standing tall over the city!

TOUR
ATHENS
Greece

The Parthenon

▶ Athens, the capital city of Greece, was named after Athena, the mythological goddess of wisdom and civilization. A more fitting patron could not have been chosen, as Athens was the birthplace of European philosophy, democracy, and theater. Ancient Greece is sometimes called the "cradle of western civilization"!

Atop the Acropolis
Dominating Athens today as it has for 2,500 years is the Parthenon, the grand temple built to honor Athena. It's considered the finest example of ancient Greek architecture. It's located on the Acropolis of Athens, which is a flat-topped rock that rises high above the city like a mountain. The word *acropolis* means "highest point of the city" in Greek.

The Parthenon actually wasn't the first building to sit on top of the Acropolis. The earlier buildings were destroyed by time, weather, and war. Before the Athenians built the Parthenon, they buried the ruins of those older buildings.

Wear and tear
The Parthenon remained in good shape for over a thousand years. It went through a lot of changes—for a while, it became a treasury, then a church, and then later a mosque.

But the Parthenon was seriously damaged during a war in 1687. Many of the beautiful marble carvings and sculptures were ruined! Some of the remaining sculptures were removed from the Parthenon and are now found in museums around the world, though many Greeks want them back, to put in their own Acropolis Museum.

Today's Athens
Today's Athens is a bustling city, a center of finance and industry. The city hosted the 2004 Summer Olympics—which was a homecoming, because the first modern Olympics were held there in 1896. The original Olympics began in Greece (though in Olympia, not in Athens) more than 2,500 years ago!

A statue of the Greek goddess Athena

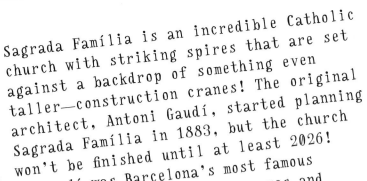

3-D POSTCARD

Sagrada Família Basilica

Barcelona, Spain

⭐ *You'll find Barcelona on the map on page 48.*

Sagrada Família is an incredible Catholic church with striking spires that are set against a backdrop of something even taller—construction cranes! The original architect, Antoni Gaudí, started planning Sagrada Família in 1883, but the church won't be finished until at least 2026!

Gaudí was Barcelona's most famous architect, known for using curves and natural shapes in his designs. After his death, his plans for the church were lost during a war. Today's Sagrada Família is the work of many other architects all trying to fulfill Gaudí's vision.

MOSCOW

Russia

St. Basil's Cathedral

The Kremlin from the Moscow River

▶ Moscow, the capital of Russia, has about 10.4 million inhabitants. That makes it the most populated city in Europe!

Red Square is the central square of Moscow, and because Moscow is the capital of Russia, it's like the central square of the entire country. The government offices are located there inside a historic walled fortress called the Kremlin, but Red Square was a gathering place for Russians long before the government moved in.

What's so red about Red Square?

There are a lot of reddish-brown bricks in the walls of Red Square, but they have nothing to do with how the square got its name. It's called Red Square because its name in Russian, *Krasnaya Ploschad* (KRAZ-nigh-uh PLAW-shad), has a different meaning in modern Russian than it did in old Russian. In old Russian, *krasnaya* meant "beautiful," but in modern Russian, it means "red." (*Ploschad* means "square.") So Red Square was originally Beautiful Square, but it came to be called Red Square.

The beauty of St. Basil's

There is something very beautiful on Red Square. It's called St. Basil's Cathedral, and it looks like a castle in a fairy tale, as you can see in the photo on the left! The architecture is a mixture of Asian and European styles, which is symbolic because Russia is partially in Europe and partially in Asia.

Next to St. Basil's Cathedral are the walls of the Kremlin. They stretch down an entire side of the square. The walls surround palaces, towers, the Russian president's home, a bell tower, and four cathedrals!

Welcome to ASIA!

More than half the world's people live in Asia, the largest continent on Earth. Asia is so vast and each region is so unique that there are tremendous differences in wealth, religion, and lifestyle. In Japan, there are watermelons that cost $20, while in the tiny island country of East Timor (near Indonesia), a family might live for a week on that sum. What else will you find in Asia? Look below for a little taste . . . then turn the page to start your tour!

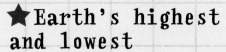

★ Earth's highest and lowest

In Asia, you'll find both the lowest land on Earth, the shores of the Dead Sea, and the highest point on Earth, Mount Everest.

★ No car? Not unusual!

In China, many people (both rich and poor) ride bicycles instead of driving cars, while in the cities of India, Pakistan, and Thailand, it is common to take a tuk-tuk taxi, which is like an enclosed motorized scooter. In parts of Asia, taxis are sometimes three-wheeled bicycles.

★ Keep out!

Bhutan, a small country in the Himalayan mountains, keeps foreign influences out so it can maintain its traditional culture. Only a limited number of tourists can visit each year, and television and the Internet have been allowed only since 1999!

★ No gum allowed

Chewing gum was totally banned in the country of Singapore from 1992 to 2004. Why? Vandals were sticking gum on trains and on elevator buttons, and it was really costly to remove it. Today "therapeutic" gum is allowed, such as the kind that strengthens enamel on teeth.

ASIA

POLITICAL MAP

20°W · 60°N · 0° · 40°E · 60°E · 80°E · 100°E · 120°E · 140°E · 160°E · 160°W · 80°N · 60°N · 40°N · 160°W

ARCTIC CIRCLE

Arctic Ocean

180°

EUROPE

Mediterranean Sea

EUROPE
ASIA

R U S S I A

Sea of Okhotsk

TURKEY
GEORGIA
ARMENIA
LEBANON
SYRIA
ISRAEL
JORDAN
AZERBAIJAN
IRAQ
KUWAIT
IRAN
BAHRAIN
QATAR
SAUDI ARABIA
YEMEN
OMAN
UNITED ARAB EMIRATES

KAZAKHSTAN

UZBEKISTAN

TURKMENISTAN
KYRGYZSTAN
TAJIKISTAN
AFGHANISTAN

PAKISTAN

MONGOLIA

NORTH KOREA
SOUTH KOREA

JAPAN

TROPIC OF CANCER

160°E

20°N

C H I N A

East China Sea

Pacific Ocean

TAIWAN

AFRICA

Arabian Sea

I N D I A

NEPAL
BHUTAN

MYANMAR
(BURMA)

BANGLADESH

LAOS

THAILAND
VIETNAM
CAMBODIA

South China Sea

PHILIPPINES

SRI LANKA

BRUNEI

EQUATOR

MALDIVES

Indian Ocean

SINGAPORE

MALAYSIA

I N D O N E S I A

EAST TIMOR

AUSTRALIA

0°

1000 Miles

0   1000   2000 Kilometers

60°E · 80°E · 100°E · 120°E · 140°E

56

A temple in Bagan, Myanmar

The orangutan is native to Indonesia and Malaysia. The name means "man of the forest" in Indonesian and Malay.

3-D PHYSICAL MAP

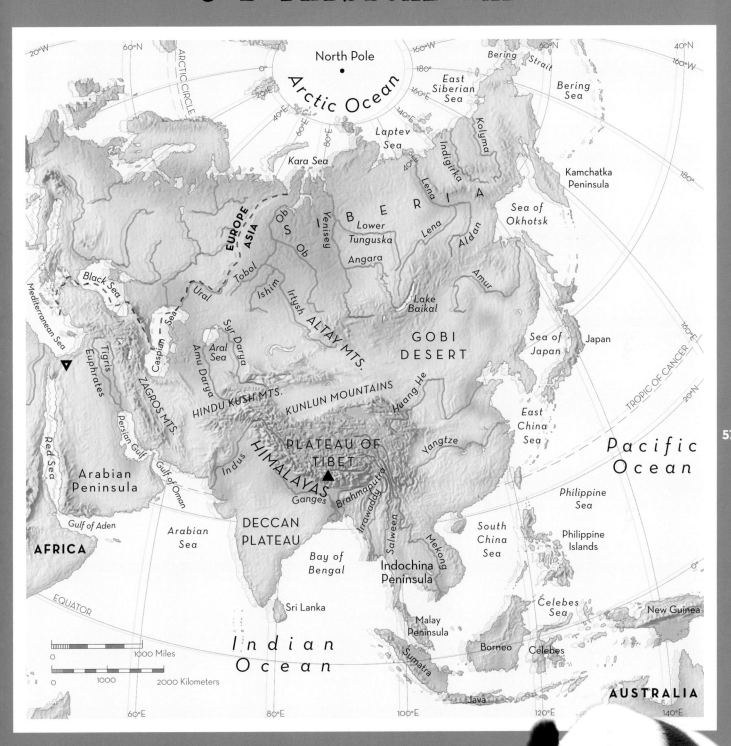

North Pole

Arctic Ocean

ARCTIC CIRCLE

EUROPE
ASIA

Bering Strait

Bering Sea

East Siberian Sea

Laptev Sea

Kara Sea

Kamchatka Peninsula

S I B E R I A

Lower Tunguska

Ob

Yenisey

Lena

Indigirka

Kolyma

Aldan

Amur

Sea of Okhotsk

Ob

Tobol

Ishim

Irtysh

ALTAY MTS.

Angara

Lake Baikal

GOBI DESERT

Sea of Japan

Japan

Black Sea

Ural

Aral Sea

Syr Darya

Amu Darya

Caspian Sea

Mediterranean Sea

Tigris

Euphrates

ZAGROS MTS.

HINDU KUSH MTS.

KUNLUN MOUNTAINS

Huang He

Yangtze

East China Sea

Persian Gulf

Red Sea

Gulf of Oman

Gulf of Aden

Arabian Peninsula

Arabian Sea

PLATEAU OF TIBET

HIMALAYAS ▲

Indus

Ganges

Brahmaputra

Irrawaddy

Salween

Mekong

Pacific Ocean

TROPIC OF CANCER

Philippine Sea

DECCAN PLATEAU

Bay of Bengal

Indochina Peninsula

South China Sea

Philippine Islands

AFRICA

EQUATOR

Sri Lanka

Malay Peninsula

Borneo

Celebes Sea

Celebes

New Guinea

Indian Ocean

Sumatra

Java

AUSTRALIA

0 — 1000 Miles

0 — 1000 — 2000 Kilometers

20°W 60°N 0° 40°E 60°E 80°E 160°W 180° 160°E 60°N 40°N 160°W
60°E 80°E 100°E 120°E 140°E 180° 160°E 0° 20°N

57

The giant panda is native to China.

MIDDLE EAST

POLITICAL MAP

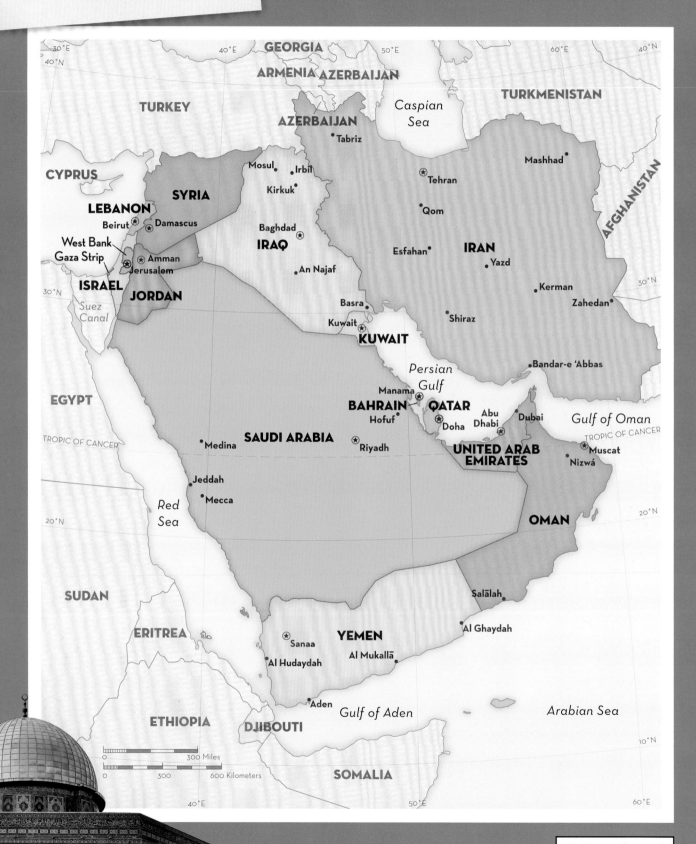

GEORGIA
ARMENIA AZERBAIJAN
TURKEY
AZERBAIJAN
Caspian Sea
TURKMENISTAN

• Tabriz
Mosul •
Mashhad •
CYPRUS
SYRIA
• Irbil
Kirkuk •
⊛ Tehran
AFGHANISTAN
LEBANON
Beirut ⊛ • Damascus
Baghdad ⊛
• Qom
West Bank
IRAQ
Gaza Strip
⊛ Amman
Jerusalem
ISRAEL
JORDAN
• An Najaf
Esfahan •
IRAN
• Yazd
• Kerman
Zahedan •
Suez Canal
Basra •
Kuwait •
Shiraz •
Bandar-e 'Abbas •
KUWAIT
Persian Gulf
EGYPT
Manama •
BAHRAIN
Hofuf •
QATAR
• Doha
Abu Dhabi •
• Dubai
Gulf of Oman
Muscat ⊛
UNITED ARAB EMIRATES
Nizwā •
SAUDI ARABIA
Riyadh ⊛
• Medina
Jeddah •
• Mecca
Red Sea
OMAN
SUDAN
Salālah •
ERITREA
Al Ghaydah •
Sanaa ⊛
YEMEN
Al Mukallā •
Al Hudaydah •
• Aden
Gulf of Aden
Arabian Sea
ETHIOPIA
DJIBOUTI
SOMALIA

TROPIC OF CANCER
TROPIC OF CANCER

30°N
20°N
10°N
30°N
20°N

30°E 40°E 50°E 60°E 40°N 50°E 60°E

0   300 Miles
0   300   600 Kilometers

⊛ National capital
• Other major city

The Dome of the Rock, an Islamic shrine in Jerusalem, Israel

Ski Dubai's indoor slopes

Ski Dubai's building

▶ Want to go skiing in the middle of a shopping mall in the desert? Want to stay in the tallest hotel in the world? Or visit an island that's shaped like a palm tree? Then head for Dubai!

Glamour in the desert

Dubai is the capital city of an emirate, or state, that is also called Dubai. It's one of seven emirates that make up the United Arab Emirates, a country on the Arabian Peninsula. The Middle East is home to some of the oldest civilizations in history, but the glitzy seaside city of Dubai features some of the most futuristic architecture and modern shopping malls on Earth!

Ski at the mall!

Dubai has the biggest mall in the Middle East, the Mall of the Emirates, and it's home to an indoor ski area with five snowy slopes!

Other famous landmarks include the World, a group of man-made islands shaped like a map of the continents, and the Palm Islands, three man-made islands shaped like palm trees. And there's the world's tallest hotel, Burj Al Arab, which is shaped like a sail and sits on its own private island. The cost to stay there? More than $1,000 per night!

Inside the Burj Al Arab hotel

The Burj Al Arab hotel

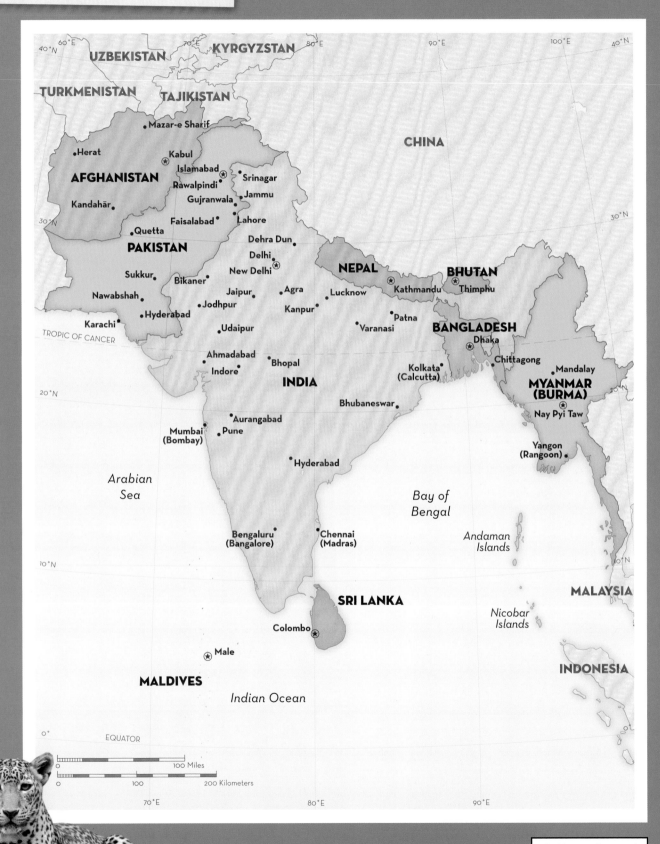

UZBEKISTAN

KYRGYZSTAN

TURKMENISTAN

TAJIKISTAN

• Mazar-e Sharif

CHINA

• Herat

• Kabul

Islamabad ⊛

AFGHANISTAN

Rawalpindi •

• Srinagar

• Jammu

Gujranwala •

Kandahār •

Faisalabad •

• Lahore

• Quetta

Dehra Dun •

PAKISTAN

Delhi •

NEPAL

BHUTAN

Sukkur •

New Delhi ⊛

⊛ Kathmandu

• Thimphu

Nawabshah •

• Bikaner

Jaipur •

• Agra

• Lucknow

• Jodhpur

Kanpur •

• Patna

BANGLADESH

• Hyderabad

Karachi •

• Udaipur

• Varanasi

Dhaka ⊛

TROPIC OF CANCER

Ahmadabad •

• Bhopal

Kolkata
(Calcutta) •

• Chittagong

• Mandalay

Indore •

INDIA

MYANMAR
(BURMA)

• Bhubaneswar

• Nay Pyi Taw

Mumbai
(Bombay) •

• Aurangabad

• Pune

Arabian
Sea

• Hyderabad

Bay of
Bengal

Yangon
(Rangoon) •

Andaman
Islands

Bengaluru
(Bangalore) •

• Chennai
(Madras)

MALAYSIA

SRI LANKA

Nicobar
Islands

Colombo ⊛

⊛ Male

INDONESIA

MALDIVES

Indian Ocean

EQUATOR

| 0 | | 100 Miles |
| 0 | 100 | 200 Kilometers |

60

South Asia is home to many big, beautiful
cats, like this leopard from Sri Lanka.

THE TAJ MAHAL

Agra, India

▶ A thousand elephants are said to have carried white marble building blocks for 186 miles (300 km) to create northern India's architectural masterpiece, the spectacular Taj Mahal.

A monument to love

As legend goes, over 350 years ago, Mughal emperor Shah Jahan had the Taj Mahal built as a monument to his beloved wife, Mumtaz, who died while giving birth to their fourteenth child. The complex took 22 years and 20,000 workers to build, at a time when the Mughal empire was failing and could not afford expensive projects. Shah Jahan's son Aurangzeb is said to have overthrown his father. Why? He thought the empire was being neglected in favor of architecture!

A change of plans

The Taj Mahal is perfectly symmetrical, except for one thing. It was designed to have one tomb—that of Mumtaz Mahal—directly beneath the dome, with other royal tombs housed in the four corner rooms.

But when Shah Jahan died, Aurangzeb decided to place his father's tomb right beside Mumtaz's tomb. This ruins the otherwise flawless symmetry of the Taj Mahal, but Shah Jahan is next to his wife for all eternity.

Today, the Taj Mahal, located in the city of Agra, is India's most popular tourist destination, visited by millions of people each year.

NEPAL

Mt. Everest

▶ The people of Nepal say *namaste* (NAH-mah-stay) when they want to welcome someone, and you're sure to hear that word plenty of times during a visit to Nepal. The Nepalese are famous for their warm hospitality. They welcome tourists to visit their capital city, Kathmandu, and to hike (or "trek") through Nepal's valleys and mountains.

Terrific treks

Eight of the world's tallest mountains, including Mount Everest, and the world's highest mountain range, the Himalayas, are in Nepal. But most people don't go to Nepal to climb to the tops of these mountains. They go to trek on the trails below, such as one called the Annapurna Circuit—a 186-mile (300-km) trail around the Annapurna mountains. Trekkers usually spend about three weeks walking the trail, staying nights in village guesthouses or in tents.

Natural mountaineers

Those who do come to climb mountains often hire Nepalese guides called Sherpas (a name that means "people of the east"). Sherpas are known for their strength at high altitudes, where the air is thin.

Tenzing Norgay is the most famous Sherpa, because in 1953 he and New Zealander Edmund Hillary were the first men to reach the top of Mount Everest. Other famous climbers have skied, snowboarded, or paraglided their way down the mountain!

A Kathmandu temple with prayer flags

62

3-D POSTCARD

The Himalayas

⭐ You'll find the Himalayas on the map on page 57.

HIMALAYAS
NEPAL

Travelers from all over the world trek in the Himalayas, and some take their adventures a step farther by climbing one of the peaks. This one is Island Peak, known in Nepal as Imja Tse, with a summit at 20,305 feet (6,189 m). During the climb, mountaineers can enjoy great views of Mount Everest, as well as Lhotse and Makalu, the world's fourth and fifth tallest mountains.

SOUTHEAST ASIA

POLITICAL MAP

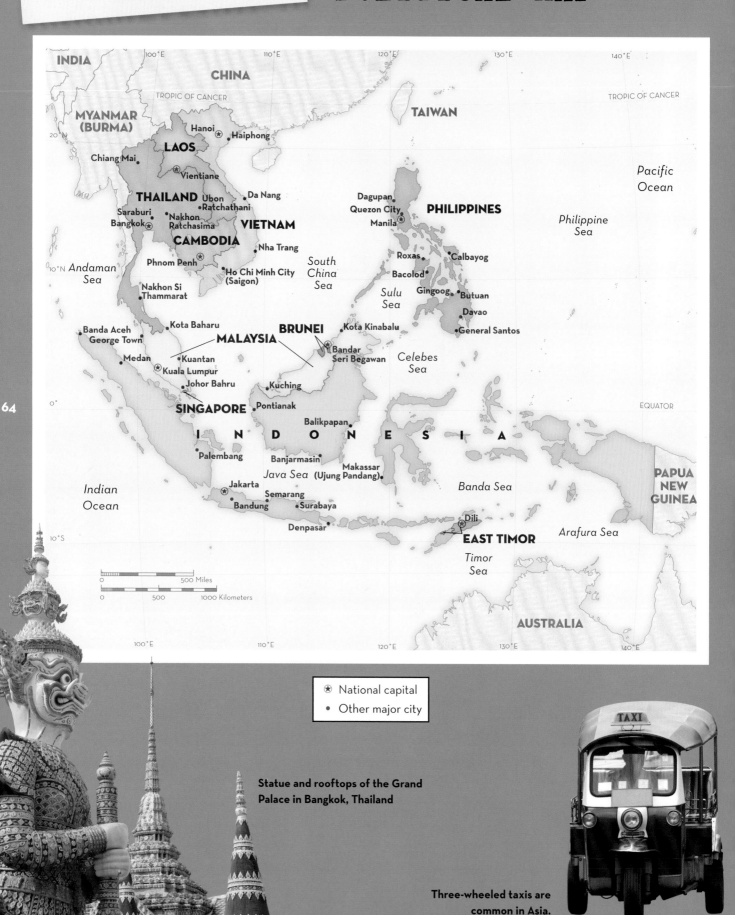

INDIA

CHINA

TROPIC OF CANCER

MYANMAR
(BURMA)

LAOS

Hanoi • • Haiphong

Chiang Mai •

• Vientiane

TAIWAN

TROPIC OF CANCER

Pacific
Ocean

THAILAND   Ubon   • Da Nang
            Ratchathani

Saraburi •
Bangkok ⊛ • Nakhon
              Ratchasima   VIETNAM

CAMBODIA

Phnom Penh ⊛   • Nha Trang

• Ho Chi Minh City
  (Saigon)

South
China
Sea

Dagupan •
Quezon City •
Manila •

PHILIPPINES

Philippine
Sea

Nakhon Si •
Thammarat

Roxas •   • Calbayog

Bacolod •

Sulu
Sea   Gingoog • • Butuan

Davao •

Andaman
Sea

Banda Aceh •
George Town •

• Kota Baharu

MALAYSIA   BRUNEI

• Kota Kinabalu

• General Santos

Medan •

• Kuantan

Kuala Lumpur ⊛

Bandar
Seri Begawan ⊛

Celebes
Sea

• Johor Bahru

• Kuching

SINGAPORE   • Pontianak

I N D O N E S I A

EQUATOR

• Balikpapan

Palembang •

• Banjarmasin

Java Sea   • Makassar
            (Ujung Pandang)

Banda Sea

PAPUA
NEW
GUINEA

Indian
Ocean

Jakarta ⊛   • Semarang

Bandung •   • Surabaya

• Denpasar

• Dili

EAST TIMOR

Arafura Sea

Timor
Sea

AUSTRALIA

0   500 Miles

0   500   1000 Kilometers

⊛ National capital

• Other major city

**Statue and rooftops of the Grand
Palace in Bangkok, Thailand**

TAXI

**Three-wheeled taxis are
common in Asia.**

3-D POSTCARD

Singapore

⭐ *You'll find Singapore on the maps on pages 56 and 64.*

Singapore is a small—but very wealthy—island nation just off the tip of the peninsula of Malaysia. Its population is a mixture of several ethnic groups, including Chinese (who make up the majority), Malay, Indian, and Arab. English is spoken as the country's common language. Lots of travelers pass through Singapore on their way around Southeast Asia, enjoying comforts of a city that is world famous for its food...and for its cleanliness!

THE TEMPLES OF ANGKOR

Cambodia

The Bayon Temple at Angkor

▶ Roughly a thousand years ago, the magnificent temples of Angkor were built by a wealthy empire called the Khmer. The Khmer built hundreds of temples, or *wats*, during their rule.

Then the Khmer empire crumbled, and the jungle grew over the temples. For many years, the city of temples was lost, a legend told among the Cambodian people living on the edge of the jungle. Finally, in 1860, a French explorer ventured into the jungle and found the Angkor temples, and then shared his discovery with the world.

Fighting back the jungle

For more than a century, French archaeologists worked to fight back the jungle and restore the temples of Angkor. And what a city they revealed! The ruins of the royal section alone, called Angkor Thom, cover 40 miles (64 km).

Angkor Wat is the most famous temple of the hundreds of temples in the area. Its towers and terraces are covered in carvings dedicated to Hindu gods, though the temple has been used by Buddhist monks for centuries.

Tourists are allowed to visit many of the temples of the Angkor region, which all feature unique details, but one favorite, Ta Prohm, has been left to the jungle. Trees grow on top of ruins, and roots intertwine with stone blocks.

The pride of Cambodia

Angkor Wat is an extraordinary work of art. With its ornate carvings and symmetrical design, it's considered an architectural masterpiece with few equals. Cambodians are so proud of Angkor Wat that it's shown on their national flag!

Angkor Wat

3-D POSTCARD

The Temples of Angkor

Cambodia

ANGKOR
CAMBODIA

Ta Prohm, one of the temples of Angkor, was built in the twelfth century as a Buddhist monastery and university. Today, it's very popular with visitors because it has not been restored. The trees that grew on top of the temple after it was abandoned are still there, so visitors can see the temple as it would have looked to the nineteenth-century explorers who found the Angkor temples in the jungle.

EAST ASIA

POLITICAL MAP

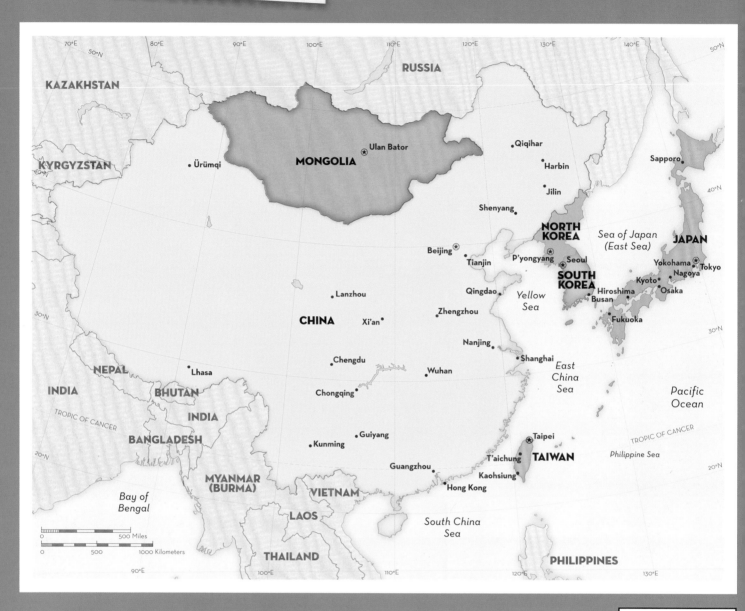

KAZAKHSTAN

RUSSIA

KYRGYZSTAN

• Ürümqi

MONGOLIA   ⊛ Ulan Bator

• Qiqihar

• Harbin

• Jilin

Shenyang •

Beijing ⊛
Tianjin •

NORTH KOREA

Sea of Japan (East Sea)

Sapporo •

JAPAN

P'yongyang ⊛   Seoul ⊛
SOUTH KOREA

Yokohama • Tokyo ⊛
Kyoto • Nagoya •
Hiroshima •   Osaka •
Busan •

Fukuoka •

• Lanzhou

Qingdao •

Yellow Sea

CHINA   Xi'an •

• Zhengzhou

NEPAL

• Lhasa

• Chengdu

• Nanjing

• Shanghai

East China Sea

Pacific Ocean

INDIA

BHUTAN

• Chongqing

• Wuhan

INDIA

TROPIC OF CANCER

BANGLADESH

• Kunming

• Guiyang

• Guangzhou

TROPIC OF CANCER

Philippine Sea

MYANMAR (BURMA)

Bay of Bengal

VIETNAM

• Taipei ⊛

T'aichung •   **TAIWAN**

Kaohsiung •
Hong Kong •

LAOS

South China Sea

THAILAND

PHILIPPINES

0   500 Miles
0   500   1000 Kilometers

⊛ National capital
• Other major city

The throne hall of Kyongbok Palace in Seoul, South Korea

Mount Fuji, the highest mountain in Japan, is a dormant volcano.

3-D POSTCARD

Hong Kong
China

⭐ *You'll find Hong Kong on the map on page 68.*

The stacks of shipping containers you see here are waiting to be loaded onto ships at the port of Hong Kong, one of the world's busiest ports.

Hong Kong is a small region of islands and coastal territories, known officially as the Special Administrative Region of Hong Kong. It was a British colony from 1842 to 1997, during which time it became an important center of trade and finance. When you see a label that says "Made in China," there's a good chance that item came through the port of Hong Kong.

THE GREAT WALL OF CHINA

China

▶ Can astronauts see the Great Wall from space? Er, not exactly. Only if the conditions are perfectly clear, they know exactly where to look, and they have really good binoculars.

But why not? Isn't the Great Wall of China the world's longest man-made structure, one that could stretch from New York to Paris? Yes, but it's only as wide as a small house. Astronauts report being able to see many other man-made structures from low orbits, but they can see the Great Wall only with help from radar or magnification.

Keep out!

The original wall was built more than 2,000 years ago by hundreds of thousands of workers over a decade, but it was rebuilt and expanded over the centuries. It was meant to keep out raiders, but it failed in that respect. How come? Invaders simply bribed the guards and crossed the wall.

The Great Wall *was* effective for communication and transportation. It was an elevated highway for soldiers who would otherwise have had to make their way over harsh mountainous terrain. And a series of watchtowers along the wall were manned by sentries with signal fires, who could quickly relay news through smoke signals.

A new kind of invader

Parts of the Great Wall have crumbled over time, while others have been rebuilt. Many people hike the wall, pacing through history as they walk past decaying watchtowers. But don't expect to see only foreign tourists. Today's China is the most populated country on Earth, and the most famous sections of the Great Wall are mobbed with Chinese tourists!

Welcome to AFRICA!

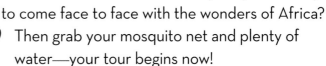

Elephants, giraffes, and lions—oh yes, Africa's got 'em. But the world's second-largest continent is *also* home to busy cities, ancient wonders, vibrant cultures, and more than 800 languages. While some African countries struggle with poverty, disease, and corruption, the continent is also full of wonderful arts and music. It's a land of great diversity, where some live in mud huts and others live in modern skyscrapers. Ready to come face to face with the wonders of Africa? Then grab your mosquito net and plenty of water—your tour begins now!

★ Ancient skeletons

Africa is sometimes called "the cradle of humanity" because the oldest human skeletons were found there, in East Africa.

★ See you at the top!

East Africa is home to snow-capped Mount Kilimanjaro, the continent's tallest mountain. People without mountain-climbing experience can attempt to climb it as long as they're in good shape.

★ Sled on the sand dunes of Namibia

In Namibia, there are giant sand dunes that you can sled down on a piece of board! (Wear a helmet.) And strangely, the dunes are next to a town where people speak German (because Namibia was once a German colony).

★ No dishes!

On the African Horn (where Ethiopia, Eritrea, Djibouti, and Somalia poke out into the sea), most people don't use forks or plates. Food sits on a flat bread called *injera* (in-JEER-ah), and this bread is also used to scoop up food, like a spoon. That means no dishes to wash!

AFRICA
POLITICAL MAP

EUROPE

ASIA

Mediterranean Sea

Madeira **(PORTUGAL)**

Canary Is. **(SPAIN)**

Rabat · Oran · Algiers · Tunis
Casablanca

MOROCCO **TUNISIA** Tripoli

Western Sahara **(MOROCCO)**

ALGERIA **LIBYA**

Alexandria
Cairo Suez

EGYPT

Red Sea

TROPIC OF CANCER

MAURITANIA
Nouakchott

Dakar **SEN. GAM.**
Banjul **G-B**
Bissau **GUINEA**
Conakry **S.L.**
Freetown
Monrovia
LIBERIA

MALI
· Timbuktu

Bamako
B.F.
Ouagadougou
GHA.
CÔTE
D'IVOIRE
Yamoussoukro
Abidjan Accra

Niamey
BEN.
TO.

NIGER

NIGERIA
Ilorin
Lagos
Porto-Novo
Lomé

CHAD
N'Djamena

· Kano
Abuja

Khartoum

SUDAN

ERITREA
Asmara

DJIBOUTI
Djibouti

Addis Ababa

ETHIOPIA

SOMALIA
Mogadishu

CAMEROON
Douala
Yaoundé

CENTRAL
AFRICAN
REPUBLIC
Bangui

UGANDA
Kisangani
Kampala

KENYA
Nairobi

EQUATOR

EQUATORIAL GUINEA

SAO TOME & PRINCIPE

Libreville

GABON **CONGO**

Brazzaville

Cabinda **(ANGOLA)**

DEMOCRATIC
REPUBLIC
OF THE CONGO

Kinshasa

Kanaga

Kigali
RWANDA
BURUNDI
Bujumbura

Dodoma
TANZANIA

Mombasa

Dar es Salaam

SEYCHELLES

Luanda

Lubumbashi

COMOROS

Atlantic
Ocean

ANGOLA

ZAMBIA
Lusaka

MALAWI
Lilongwe

NAMIBIA

ZIMBABWE
Harare

MOZAMBIQUE

Antananarivo

MAURITIUS

MADAGASCAR

Réunion **(FRANCE)**

Windhoek

BOTSWANA
Gaborone

TROPIC OF CAPRICORN

Pretoria
Maputo
Johannesburg Mbabane
Bloemfontein **SWAZILAND**
Maseru Durban
SOUTH **LESOTHO**
AFRICA
Cape Town · Port Elizabeth

Indian
Ocean

0 500 Miles

0 500 1000 Kilometers

Hassan II Mosque in Casablanca, Morocco

⊛ National capital

· Other major city

Note: South Africa has three capitals because its government is spread out among three cities.

B.F.	BURKINA FASO
BEN.	BENIN
G-B	GUINEA-BISSAU
GAM.	GAMBIA
GHA.	GHANA
S.L.	SIERRA LEONE
SEN.	SENEGAL
TO.	TOGO

3-D PHYSICAL MAP

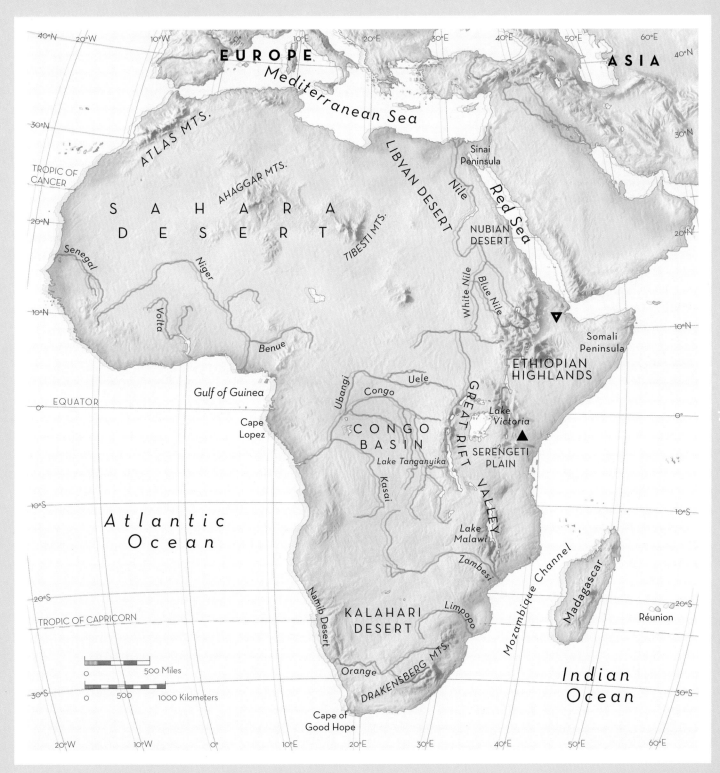

EUROPE

ASIA

Mediterranean Sea

ATLAS MTS.

TROPIC OF CANCER

S A H A R A   D E S E R T

AHAGGAR MTS.

Senegal

Niger

Volta

Benue

TIBESTI MTS.

LIBYAN DESERT

Sinai Peninsula

Nile

Red Sea

NUBIAN DESERT

White Nile

Blue Nile

▽

Somali Peninsula

ETHIOPIAN HIGHLANDS

Gulf of Guinea

Cape Lopez

Ubangi

Congo

Uele

GREAT RIFT VALLEY

Lake Victoria

▲

SERENGETI PLAIN

EQUATOR

CONGO BASIN

Lake Tanganyika

Kasai

Atlantic Ocean

Lake Malawi

Zambesi

Madagascar

Réunion

Namib Desert

KALAHARI DESERT

Limpopo

Mozambique Channel

Indian Ocean

TROPIC OF CAPRICORN

Orange

DRAKENSBERG MTS.

Cape of Good Hope

500 Miles

500   1000 Kilometers

MAP KEY

▲ HIGHEST POINT: Mount Kilimanjaro, Tanzania, *elevation 19,340 feet (5,895 m)*

▼ LOWEST POINT: Lake Assal, Djibouti, *elevation –512 feet (–156 m)*

Mount Kilimanjaro, Tanzania

TOUR

THE NILE RIVER

Northeastern Africa

But the river has parasites, and sometimes there are crocodiles, so swimming isn't such a great idea.

In Uganda, the Nile region is home to *lots* of crocodiles and to an incredible variety of birds and hundreds of hippos. Hippos are vegetarian, but they have 4-inch-wide (10-cm) teeth and won't hesitate to use them in self-defense. So never get between a hippo and the water, as that gets them all riled up. Oh, and don't stand around when a hippo marks its territory—the hippo uses its tail to fling poop everywhere!

74

The Nile River creates a winding ribbon of green that cuts through the desert in Egypt. In ancient times, Egypt became a great civilization because the Nile flooded over its banks once a year, making farmlands fertile and bringing food and life to the desert.

But the Nile isn't only in Egypt. It's the longest river in the world, flowing more than half the length of Africa on its way to the Mediterranean.

Watch out for crocs and hippos!

In Egypt, the southern Nile is lined with *feluccas* (feh-LOO-kuhz), a type of sailboat used since ancient times to travel the river. Today's *feluccas* are full of tourists, who visit temples alongside the river and sleep on the boats. Some tourists swim in the Nile when the weather is hot, just like local people do.

Move that temple

The Nile used to flood every year when snow in the mountains of Ethiopia melted. Why doesn't it flood anymore? Because the Egyptians built the Aswan High Dam in the 1960s. This controlled water levels and created electricity, but the huge lake that was created behind it flooded homes and ancient temples.

Thousands of people had to move, and some of the ancient sites did, too. Some temples were carefully moved, piece by piece, to higher ground. The Temple of Dendur went all the way to the Metropolitan Museum in New York City!

A felucca on the Nile

3-D POSTCARD
The Great Pyramids
Giza, Egypt

⭐ You'll find Giza on the map on page 74.

GREAT PYRAMIDS
EGYPT

Standing tall for more than 4,000 years, the three huge pyramids of Giza were built as tombs for pharaohs.

Here you can see Khafre's pyramid, the second largest of the three. In front of the pyramids is the Great Sphinx, a statue of a mythological creature that's half man and half lion. The Sphinx is supposed to guard the pyramids. No one knows what happened to the Sphinx's nose. It's been missing for hundreds of years!

THE SAHARA DESERT

North Africa

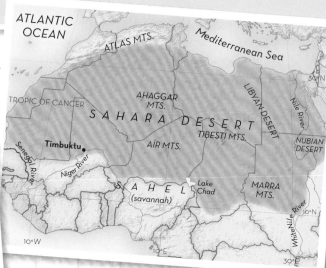

The word *sahara* means "desert" in Arabic. And what a desert it is! The Sahara is the hottest place on Earth, and it almost never rains there. It covers one-third of Africa, and it's almost the same size as the entire United States.

Mountains of sand

The most famous images of the Sahara are of huge yellow and orange sand dunes. Some of these dunes are so big that they are stationary, like mountains, but other dunes change with the wind. Not all of the Sahara is sand, though— much of it is covered in gravel or rock.

The Sahara may be the world's largest hot desert, but at night it's freezing cold. Why? Because there's nothing to retain the heat. In wetter places, plants and water get heated up by the sun during the day, and at night they slowly release this heat. Since the Sahara is so dry and plantless, it cools down fast when the sun sets!

How does anything survive?

Most people who live in the Sahara live in cities or towns that sit by a source of water. But there are some nomads (people who live on the move) in the harsh desert. These people survive with the help of camels. They ride camels, eat camel meat, drink camel milk, and use camel skin. Camels are very well suited to living in the desert, because they can conserve water in their bodies, and they can nourish themselves on the fat in their humps when food is scarce.

3-D POSTCARD

Timbuktu

Mali

⭐ *You'll find Timbuktu on the maps on pages 72 and 76.*

TIMBUKTU MALI

When people talk about something really far away, they say it's as far as Timbuktu. But did you know that Timbuktu is a real city? It's in the Sahara Desert in Mali, a country in West Africa. Eight hundred years ago, Timbuktu was a wealthy trading city, famous for trade in salt and gold, but today it's known for its ancient mud-brick mosques and buildings.

TOUR

THE GREAT RIFT VALLEY

East Africa

Two Maasai boys

There's a giant crack in the earth that goes all the way from the Arabian Peninsula to southeastern Africa! It's called the Great Rift Valley, but really, it's not just a single valley. It's a whole region, and within it there are mountains and volcanoes, lush safari lands full of animals, archaeological sites, steep cliffs, craters, and deep lakes.

Safari, anyone?

The most famous parts of the Great Rift Valley are in Kenya and Tanzania, where thousands of animals live. Tourists come from all over the world to visit dozens of national parks in and around the Rift Valley. Once tourists came to hunt big animals, but now they come to shoot only with their cameras.

The most popular animals to photograph are called the Big Five: lions, buffalos, rhinos, elephants, and leopards.

But there are hundreds of other animals that cannot be found in the wild anywhere outside of Africa—like hippos, zebras, giraffes, gorillas, warthogs, and wildebeests. These animals roam

a region of grassy plains called the Serengeti (a name that means "endless plain"), enjoying the plentiful food and water. Massive herds of animals run free while tourists are confined to camps, settlements, and cars.

Jump for joy!

People also live in the Great Rift Valley, and not just in the cities. There are small villages where tribes of people live in mud huts. Some of these people are called Maasai (MAH-sigh). They dress in red blankets, use spears and sticks to keep lions away, and herd cattle. They are famous for expressing their joy by leaping straight into the air. You can tell how rich a Maasai man is by the number of cows he owns!

78

3-D POSTCARD

Safari!

East Africa

EAST ★ AFRICA

Jambo, twiga (JAHM-bo, TWEE-ga). That means "Hello, giraffe" in Swahili. You probably already know another word in the African language of Swahili: safari! *Safari* means "journey," but when you go on safari, it usually means taking your camera and driving around special African nature reserves where the animals roam free, while humans have to sit in the car. Here you can see a giraffe that you might see on safari in East Africa—much closer than you'd see from a car!

TOUR
CAPE TOWN
South Africa

Cape Town is a world-class city near the southern tip of Africa. It's set between coast and mountains in one of the most beautiful urban environments in the world.

A table in the clouds

Cape Town has a very interesting mountain looming nearby—it has a flat top, so it's called, fittingly, Table Mountain. Sometimes when the mountain is covered in clouds, people say that a tablecloth is on Table Mountain.

The drop down from Table Mountain to the neighborhoods in the foothills is steep, though some people hike the slope to the top for the view. Most people take the cable car up, which slowly turns in circles as it travels.

Don't miss the boats

The most visited spot in South Africa is the Victoria & Albert Waterfront, which is an industrial seaport that has been converted into a modern shopping and office complex. Small ships are cleaned and repaired here, right in view of shoppers, who might even have to wait for the "swing bridge" to pivot back over the water after it has swung aside to allow boats to cross.

From the V&A Waterfront, you can catch the ferry to Robben Island Museum, a former prison 7.5 miles (12 km) offshore near Cape Town. That's where Nelson Mandela was held prisoner for 27 years for believing that the government's policy called *apartheid* was wrong.

Under apartheid, descendents of European immigrants controlled the government and the economy while African natives were forced to live separately, usually in poverty. When this era ended, South Africa entered a time of great change, and Nelson Mandela was released in 1990 and elected president four years later!

Sailing toward Table Mountain in the distance.

Welcome to # AUSTRALIA & OCEANIA!

Australia, the smallest of the world's seven continents, is also the biggest landmass in a region called Oceania. Oceania is made up of thousands of islands in the southern Pacific Ocean. It includes tiny island countries in regions called Micronesia, Melanesia, and Polynesia, as well as the bigger countries of "Australasia"— Australia, New Zealand, and New Guinea. What will you find in this part of the world? Check out some highlights below!

★ How many islands? Who knows!

No one knows exactly how many islands are in Oceania. Many of the 20,000 to 30,000 islands in this part of the world are too small to show on the maps of the region!

★ Crikey!

Some people refer to Australia as "Down Under" because it's so far south. It's almost all desert, except for the coast. Most Australians— except for natives called Australian Aborigines—live on the east coast, which has tropical rain forests, cities, beaches, and a famous opera house in Sydney.

★ Not like the neighbor!

New Zealand, consisting of two main islands, is the second-biggest country in Oceania. It's totally different from Australia—it has no deserts at all. Instead, it has mountains, glaciers, caves, forests, hot springs, and more.

★ Fries with that?

New Guinea is famous for its cannibals! Some tribes claim that they still eat people today, but other tribes say that they stopped the practice about 40 years ago.

AUSTRALIA & OCEANIA

POLITICAL MAP

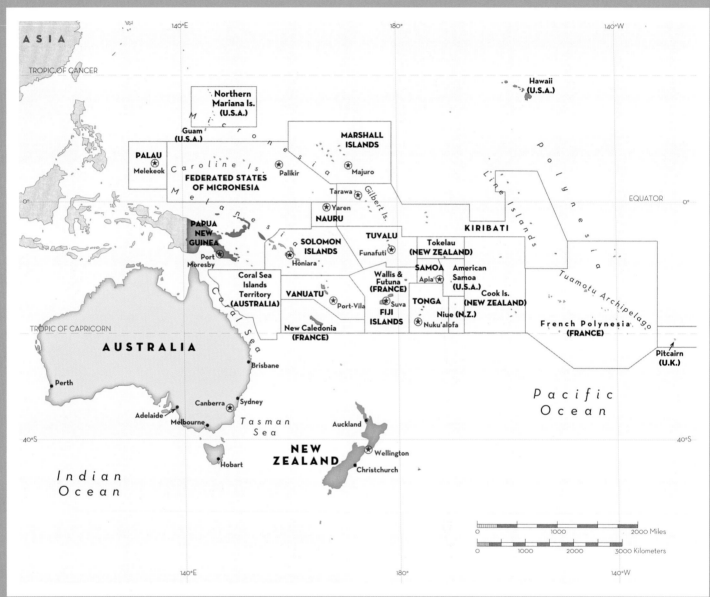

ASIA

TROPIC OF CANCER

140°E   180°   140°W

Hawaii
(U.S.A.)

Northern
Mariana Is.
(U.S.A.)

Guam
(U.S.A.)

MARSHALL
ISLANDS

Majuro

PALAU
Melekeok

Caroline Is.

FEDERATED STATES
OF MICRONESIA

Palikir

Tarawa

Gilbert Is.

Line Islands

EQUATOR

Polynesia

Micronesia

PAPUA
NEW
GUINEA

Port
Moresby

Melanesia

Yaren

NAURU

TUVALU

Funafuti

SOLOMON
ISLANDS

Honiara

KIRIBATI

Tokelau
(NEW ZEALAND)

SAMOA

Apia

American
Samoa
(U.S.A.)

Cook Is.
(NEW ZEALAND)

Tuamotu Archipelago

Coral Sea
Islands
Territory
(AUSTRALIA)

VANUATU

Port-Vila

Wallis &
Futuna
(FRANCE)

Suva

FIJI
ISLANDS

TONGA

Niue (N.Z.)

Nuku'alofa

French Polynesia
(FRANCE)

Pitcairn
(U.K.)

New Caledonia
(FRANCE)

Coral Sea

AUSTRALIA

TROPIC OF CAPRICORN

Perth

Brisbane

Canberra   Sydney

Adelaide

Melbourne

Hobart

Tasman
Sea

Auckland

NEW
ZEALAND

Wellington

Christchurch

Pacific
Ocean

Indian
Ocean

40°S   40°S

0   1000   2000 Miles

0   1000   2000   3000 Kilometers

140°E   180°   140°W

⊛ National capital
• Other major city

The skyline of Sydney, Australia

AUSTRALASIA
3-D PHYSICAL MAP

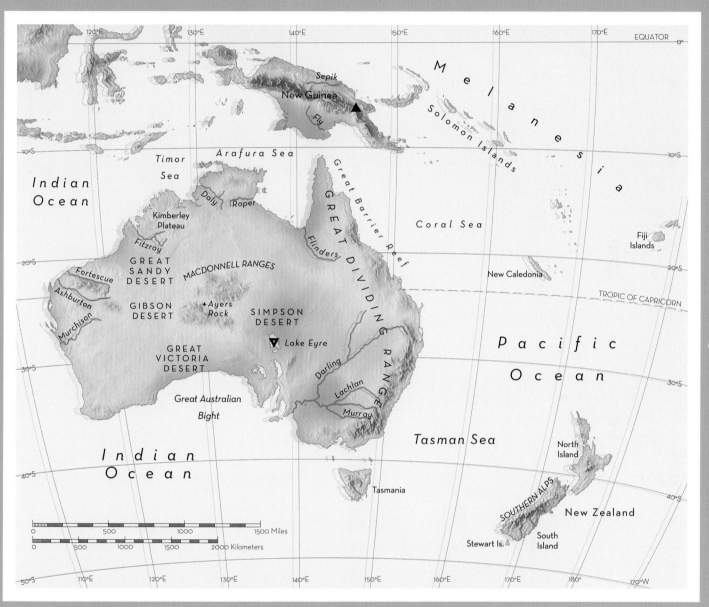

EQUATOR

Melanesia

Sepik

New Guinea

Fly

Solomon Islands

Arafura Sea

Timor Sea

Indian Ocean

Daly

Roper

Kimberley Plateau

Great Barrier Reef

Coral Sea

Fiji Islands

Fitzroy

Flinders

New Caledonia

TROPIC OF CAPRICORN

Fortescue

GREAT SANDY DESERT

MACDONNELL RANGES

Ashburton

Murchison

GIBSON DESERT

+ Ayers Rock

SIMPSON DESERT

GREAT DIVIDING RANGE

Pacific Ocean

Lake Eyre

GREAT VICTORIA DESERT

Darling

Lachlan

Great Australian Bight

Murray

Tasman Sea

North Island

Indian Ocean

Tasmania

SOUTHERN ALPS

New Zealand

Stewart Is.

South Island

500   1000   1500 Miles

500   1000   1500   2000 Kilometers

83

MAP KEY

▲ **HIGHEST POINT:**
Mount Wilhelm, Papua New Guinea,
elevation 14,793 feet (4, 509 m)

▼ **LOWEST POINT:**
Lake Eyre, Australia,
elevation -52 feet (-16 m)

"Australasia" includes
Australia, New Zealand,
and New Guinea.

**Ayers Rock in
central Australia**

THE GREAT BARRIER REEF

Australia

84

▶ Thousands of creatures live in and around Australia's Great Barrier Reef, the world's largest coral reef system. It's so big that astronauts can take photos of it from space! The photos show blue-green blobs set against a dark blue ocean—these are actually the tops of some of about 2,900 separate reefs that form Great Barrier Reef Marine Park. This park is *big*—it's the same size as Japan!

It's alive!

Coral reefs are made of limestone, which comes from skeletons of tiny sea creatures and plants. They are covered with billions of living coral animals called polyps that grow healthily

with steady sunlight and cool water. The polyps absorb more limestone as they extract it (in its dissolved form) from the ocean water. When the coral polyps die, their limestone skeletons remain and become part of the reef.

The Great Barrier Reef is home to more than just coral. A mind-boggling number of colorful fish dart among the coral branches, along with jellies, sharks, rays, turtles, starfish, sea snakes, whales, and plants. There are even 629 types of seaweed in the marine park, which are used by humans to make food, cosmetics, and even printer ink!

Respect the reef

The Great Barrier Reef is one of the most amazing underwater sights on Earth, so people travel from all around the world to see it and swim near it. Do people damage the reef? Sometimes. Not everyone realizes that reefs are alive and should be left alone. So if *you* visit, remember: look, but don't touch!

Kangaroos. These marsupials travel by hopping. Baby kangaroos are called joeys, while large male kangaroos are called boomers. Australian children are sometimes told that Santa's sleigh is pulled by six white boomers.

▶ For 50 million years, Australia was isolated from the rest of the world, so its plants and animals developed differently from animals on the other continents. Tens of thousands of years ago, Australia was home to some enormous animals called megafauna (a name that means "giant animal"). One species looked like a kangaroo but was 8 feet (2.4 m) tall. Another was a giant meat-eating lizard that was longer than a house!

Today's Australian animals are smaller, and many are marsupials, which means the females have pouches that their babies live in. On this page, you'll find some of Australia's most unique animal inhabitants!

Tasmanian devils. These meat-eaters are famous for their bad tempers. They scream to show how tough they are, and they're nature's garbage collectors, eating any meat no matter how old and rotten it is. They also eat bones and fur.

Platypuses. The shy, furry platypus has a duckbill and webbed feet. Add to this a flat, broad tail and you have an animal so bizarre that Europeans at first thought it was a joke!

Koalas. Though they're often called koala bears, these cute marsupials are not actually bears! Koalas sleep 19 hours a day and have fingerprints just like humans and primates. In fact, a koala fingerprint is almost identical to a human fingerprint.

Kookaburras. The cackle of a kookaburra sounds like a crazy laugh! The kookaburra is a tough bird that can kill and eat lizards, mice, and snakes. Kookaburras have even been known to snatch meat right off a barbecue!

TOUR
ROTORUA
New Zealand

▶ On New Zealand's North Island, in a region full of lakes and hot springs, is an entire town that stinks of rotten eggs. P-U! It's called Rotorua, but tourists call it "Rotten-rua." So why is it a top attraction of the North Island?

A steaming hot town

Rotorua is the most active geothermal area in New Zealand. *Geothermal* refers to heat that comes from underground—this heat warms gas and water below the surface, and in Rotorua, the hot gas and water can flow up to the surface. So, parts of Rotorua steam and hiss, while other parts erupt, spewing hot water as geysers.

One geyser erupts every hour, shooting 65 feet (20 m) into the air! This geyser is located in the middle of town, at an area called *Te Whakarewarewatanga o te Ope Taua a Wahiao*. This name comes from the language of the Maori, natives of New Zealand, and it means "an uprising of the Wahiao warriors." But don't worry about pronouncing that mouthful of a name—most people just call it Whaka!

What's the smell?

The rotten-egg smell comes from sulfur steaming up out of the earth. But the local Maori welcome the smell because it brings with it natural heating and cooking facilities! They can boil food by carefully dipping it into a hot pool, or cook a feast called a *hangi* by burying it in a hole full of steam.

3-D POSTCARD

Queenstown
New Zealand

⭐ You'll find Queenstown on the map on page 86.

QUEENSTOWN NEW ZEALAND

Imagine having a long, stretchy cord called a bungee (like a huge rubber band) attached to your legs, then leaping off a New Zealand bridge 141 feet (43 m) high! Imagine plunging toward a river in a beautiful gorge, getting dunked in the water, and then being snapped back up to bounce around in the air. Pretty wild! The bungee jump at Kawarau Bridge in Queenstown, New Zealand, was the world's first. Bungee jumping requires precise calculations and careful preparation—so don't try this at home!

TOUR

EASTER ISLAND

Oceania
(governed by Chile)

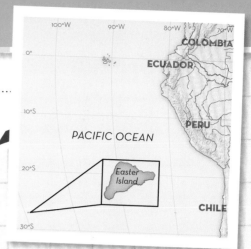

Easter Island is one of the world's most isolated islands. It's so far from its parent country, Chile, that it takes six days to get there by ship! Its nearest neighbor—Pitcairn Island—is 1,300 miles (2,000 km) away.

Easter Island is famous for having almost 900 stone statues—called *moai* (MO-eye)—and two of the world's great mysteries: How were these huge statues moved to their locations? And what happened to the people who carved them?

Hauling heads

Moai are stone head-and-torso carvings that can be as tall as a two-story house. Possibly created for ceremonial or religious purposes, they

were carved in one pit from volcanic ash stone, then hauled to different sites around Easter Island.

How were they hauled? Today's Easter Islanders have proven that the statues could have been moved on wooden platforms or rolled on rocks placed under the statues. Some researchers have demonstrated that an upright *moai* can be moved by 17 men pulling on ropes, producing a side-to-side jerking motion that makes it look like the *moai* is walking!

What happened?

What befell the civilization that created the *moai*? It seems to have met a tragic end. Did the people of isolated Easter Island damage their own environment? Did the population disappear from European diseases, or were the natives kidnapped to become slaves?

No one knows, though written tablets have been found on Easter Island. Perhaps, if the writing is someday deciphered, we'll finally understand what happened—and why the people knocked over their statues before vanishing.

Welcome to ANTARCTICA!

Antarctica is the coldest, windiest place on Earth! It's completely covered in ice, and it's so harsh and bone-chilling that people don't even live there, except for visiting scientists and workers. Tourists only travel to Antarctica during the southern summer, from November to April. They see spectacular landscapes of ice—frozen mountains, enormous white plains, and blue ice caves. Visitors and scientists usually wear sunglasses because the white glare is so bright. So, grab your specs (your 3-D specs, in this case)—it's time to visit Earth's frozen continent!

★ Incredible icebergs!
During the winter, a layer of ice forms on the sea, and Antarctica doubles in size. Sometimes big chunks of ice break off and float out into the ocean—these "chunks," better known as icebergs, can be as big as office buildings or even entire cities!

★ Bet you didn't know...
Even though Antarctica is full of frozen water, it is technically a desert. It rains less there than in the Sahara!

★ Lifeless? No way!
Antarctica may be cold and far away from the other continents, but it's not lifeless. Incredible birds, penguins, seals, and whales call Antarctica home. They all like to eat krill, tiny animals that swim in swarms in the Antarctic seas. They look like see-through lobsters the size of your pinky!

★ No passport required
No one owns Antarctica. It does not have passports or sales tax or wars. It's reserved for peace and science by the Antarctic Treaty, signed by 45 countries since 1959.

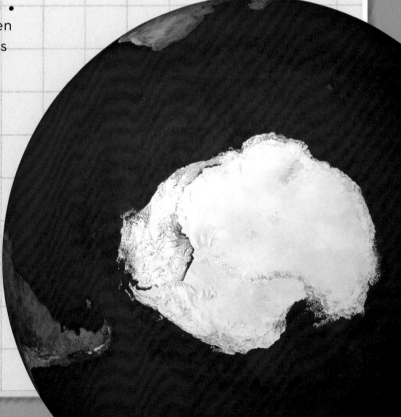

ANTARCTICA

POLITICAL MAP

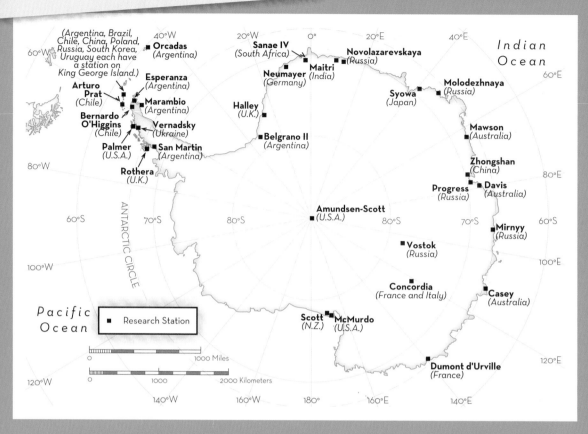

(Argentina, Brazil, Chile, China, Poland, Russia, South Korea, Uruguay each have a station on King George Island.)

- Orcadas *(Argentina)*
- Sanae IV *(South Africa)*
- Novolazarevskaya *(Russia)*
- Maitri *(India)*
- Neumayer *(Germany)*
- Esperanza *(Argentina)*
- Arturo Prat *(Chile)*
- Marambio *(Argentina)*
- Bernardo O'Higgins *(Chile)*
- Vernadsky *(Ukraine)*
- Palmer *(U.S.A.)*
- San Martin *(Argentina)*
- Rothera *(U.K.)*
- Halley *(U.K.)*
- Belgrano II *(Argentina)*
- Molodezhnaya *(Russia)*
- Syowa *(Japan)*
- Mawson *(Australia)*
- Zhongshan *(China)*
- Progress *(Russia)*
- Davis *(Australia)*
- Amundsen-Scott *(U.S.A.)*
- Mirnyy *(Russia)*
- Vostok *(Russia)*
- Concordia *(France and Italy)*
- Casey *(Australia)*
- Scott *(N.Z.)*
- McMurdo *(U.S.A.)*
- Dumont d'Urville *(France)*

Indian Ocean

Pacific Ocean

ANTARCTIC CIRCLE

- Research Station

0 — 1000 Miles

0 — 1000 — 2000 Kilometers

3-D PHYSICAL MAP

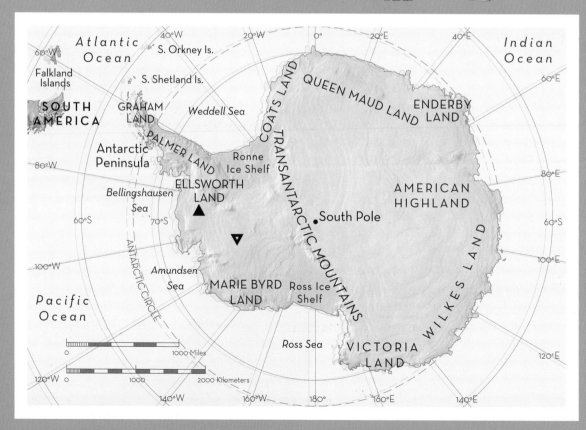

Atlantic Ocean

- Falkland Islands
- S. Orkney Is.
- S. Shetland Is.
- SOUTH AMERICA
- GRAHAM LAND
- Weddell Sea
- COATS LAND
- QUEEN MAUD LAND
- ENDERBY LAND
- *Indian Ocean*
- Antarctic Peninsula
- PALMER LAND
- Ronne Ice Shelf
- TRANSANTARCTIC MOUNTAINS
- Bellingshausen Sea
- ELLSWORTH LAND
- AMERICAN HIGHLAND
- South Pole
- Amundsen Sea
- MARIE BYRD LAND
- Ross Ice Shelf
- WILKES LAND
- *Pacific Ocean*
- Ross Sea
- VICTORIA LAND
- ANTARCTIC CIRCLE

0 — 1000 Miles

0 — 1000 — 2000 Kilometers

MAP KEY

▲ **HIGHEST POINT:**
Vinson Massif,
elevation 16,067 feet (4,897 m)

▽ **LOWEST POINT:**
Bentley Subglacial Trench,
elevation –8,383 feet (–2,555 m)

McMurdo Station

South Pole golf!

▶ No one is a permanent resident of Antarctica, but lots of people stay there for months at a time at scientific research stations. But not all these people are scientists—some of them are electricians, plumbers, carpenters, mechanics, chefs, and even cleaners. Imagine having the job of scrubbing toilets at the South Pole!

In the name of science

Four thousand people live in 30 research stations around Antarctica over the summer months, but in winter only a thousand stay on. The biggest United States research station, McMurdo Station, has fewer than 200 residents in the winter, but that figure is five times as big in the summer. The United States also operates Palmer Station and Amundsen-Scott South Pole Station—named after the first explorers to reach the South Pole.

Meet the polies

Lots of the scientists at the Amundsen-Scott South Pole Station are astronomers—the sun doesn't rise there for half the year, allowing plenty of time to study the night sky. Other scientists study earthquakes and weather.

From February to October, there are around a hundred people—nicknamed "polies"—at the Amundsen-Scott South Pole Station, and they can't dash over to the supermarket when they run out of milk or want a chocolate bar. Polies are completely isolated in the Antarctic darkness, and they rely entirely on supplies brought in during the summer months.

Living mostly inside for months, polies entertain themselves with games, movies, and trivia nights. Then, when October rolls around and there's daylight again, they can finally head outside for a game of golf or volleyball on the ice!

91

Emperor penguins

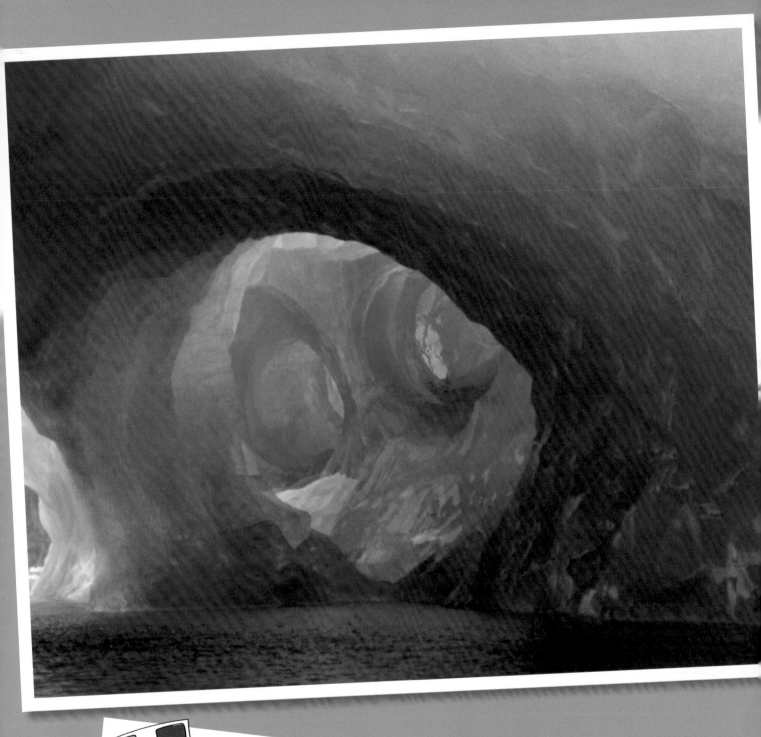

3-D POSTCARD

An Antarctic Ice Cave

ANTARCTICA

As you peek inside this cave in the Antarctic ice, do you wonder why it's blue? It's blue because that's what happens when sunlight, which is white light (a combination of all the colors of the rainbow), shines through the dense glacier ice. All the colors except blue get absorbed by the water molecules, so we see blue!

JOURNEY'S END

You've reached the end of your world tour! You've trotted the globe, covered the continents, and taken in lots of sights. But the world is a big place, too big to fit in a book. There's so much more to see—from the skyscrapers of Shanghai to the beaches of Sri Lanka to the chilly plains of Mongolia!

The highlights you've seen on your tour are only the beginning, and even though this is the *end* of the book, you now have a great start to your future adventures. Did you like some of the stops on this tour especially? Then start a list of "must-see spots in the world," and hopefully, someday, you'll get to visit every one of them!

MY must-see spots in the world:

....

....

....

....

....

....

....

WORLD POLITICAL MAP

Beaufort
Sea

Baffin
Bay

Greenland
(DENMARK)

ARCTIC CIRCLE

Alaska
(U.S.A.)

Hudson
Bay

ICE

CANADA

IRE

Gulf of
Alaska

40°N

UNITED STATES

Atlantic
Ocean

Canar
Island
(SPAIN

TROPIC OF CANCER

Gulf of
Mexico

BAHAMAS

Wester
(MORC

MEXICO

CUBA HAITI
JAMAICA
BELIZE
HONDURAS

DOMINICAN
REPUBLIC
Puerto Rico
(U.S.A.)

CAPE
VERDE
SEN
GAMBIA –
GUINEA-BISSAU
GUINE
SIERRA LE
LIE

Hawaii
(U.S.A.)

GUATEMALA
EL SALVADOR   NICARAGUA
COSTA RICA

See map on
page 26
for detail.

TRINIDAD &
TOBAGO

PANAMA
VENEZUELA
GUYANA
SURINAME
French Guiana
(FRANCE)

COLOMBIA

EQUATOR

Galápagos
Islands
(ECUADOR)

ECUADOR

BRAZIL

Pacific
Ocean

PERU

BOLIVIA

TROPIC OF CAPRICORN

PARAGUAY

CHILE

Easter
Island
(CHILE)

URUGUAY

Atlantic
Ocean

ARGENTINA

40°S

Falkland Islands
(U.K.)

South Georgia
(U.K.)

ALB.	ALBANIA
ARM.	ARMENIA
B&H	BOSNIA & HERZEGOVINA
BULG.	BULGARIA
CRO.	CROATIA
C.R.	CZECH REPUBLIC
KOS.	KOSOVO
LITH.	LITHUANIA
LUX.	LUXEMBOURG
MAC.	MACEDONIA
NETH.	NETHERLANDS
SER.	SERBIA
MON.	MONTENEGRO
SLOV.	SLOVENIA

160°W   ANTARCTIC CIRCLE 120°W   80°W   **ANTARCTICA**   40°W

Arctic Ocean

40°E
80°E
120°E
160°E

0°
80°N

Svalbard
(NORWAY)

Barents
Sea

Kara
Sea

Laptev
Sea

East
Siberian
Sea

Norwegian
Sea

ARCTIC CIRCLE

SWEDEN
FINLAND

NORWAY

North
Sea

ESTONIA

LATVIA

LITH.

RUSSIA

Sea of
Okhotsk

Bering
Sea

UNITED
KINGDOM

DENMARK

Baltic Sea

Kaliningrad (RUSSIA)

BELARUS

NETH.

POLAND

BELGIUM

GERMANY

C.R.

SLOVAKIA

UKRAINE

LUX.

AUSTRIA

HUNGARY

MOLDOVA

KAZAKHSTAN

MONGOLIA

NORTH
KOREA

SOUTH
KOREA

JAPAN

40°N

SWITZERLAND

SLOV.

ROMANIA

FRANCE

ITALY

CRO.

B&H SER.

GEORGIA

Black
Sea

MON.

BULG.

Caspian Sea

Aral
Sea

UZBEKISTAN

KYRGYZSTAN

MAC.

KOS.

ALB.

GREECE

TURKEY

ARM.

TURKMENISTAN

TAJIKISTAN

SPAIN

PORTUGAL

Mediterranean Sea

CYPRUS

SYRIA

AZERBAIJAN

CHINA

East
China
Sea

LEBANON

ISRAEL

IRAQ

JORDAN

IRAN

AFGHANISTAN

PAKISTAN

NEPAL

BHUTAN

TAIWAN

MOROCCO

TUNISIA

Red Sea

QATAR

KUWAIT

TROPIC OF CANCER

ALGERIA

LIBYA

EGYPT

SAUDI
ARABIA

UNITED ARAB
EMIRATES

BANGLADESH

INDIA

MYANMAR
(BURMA)

Pacific
Ocean

OMAN

LAOS

MAURITANIA

MALI

NIGER

CHAD

ERITREA

YEMEN

Arabian
Sea

Bay of
Bengal

THAILAND

VIETNAM

PHILIPPINES

BURKINA
FASO

SUDAN

DJIBOUTI

CAMBODIA

South
China
Sea

GHANA

NIGERIA

CENTRAL
AFRICAN
REPUBLIC

ETHIOPIA

SRI
LANKA

BRUNEI

IVORY
COAST

CAMEROON

MALDIVES

MALAYSIA

TOGO

BENIN

EQUATORIAL
GUINEA

CONGO

UGANDA

KENYA

SOMALIA

SINGAPORE

0°

GABON

DEMOCRATIC
REPUBLIC
OF THE
CONGO

RWANDA

BURUNDI

TANZANIA

SEYCHELLES

INDONESIA

PAPUA
NEW
GUINEA

See map on
page 82
for detail.

SOLOMON
ISLANDS

Cabinda
(ANGOLA)

EAST TIMOR

ANGOLA

MALAWI

Indian
Ocean

Coral
Sea

VANUATU

FIJI
ISLANDS

ZAMBIA

MOZAMBIQUE

ZIMBABWE

MADAGASCAR

MAURITIUS

New Caledonia
(FRANCE)

NAMIBIA

BOTSWANA

Réunion
(FRANCE)

AUSTRALIA

TROPIC OF CAPRICORN

SWAZILAND

SOUTH
AFRICA

LESOTHO

Tasman
Sea

40°S

NEW
ZEALAND

0   1000   2000   3000   4000 Miles

0   1000   2000   3000   4000   5000   6000 Kilometers

ANTARCTICA

0°
40°E
80°E
120°E
160°E   ANTARCTIC CIRCLE